THE STAR OF ATTÉGHÉI;

THE VISION OF SCHWARTZ;

AND

OTHER POEMS.

By FRANCES BROWN.

LONDON:

EDWARD MOXON, DOVER STREET.

MDCCCXLIV.

CONTENTS.

EDITOR'S PREFACE.

THE plea of circumstance is not admissible in the critic's court,—but is rarely without its influence in other quarters. The critic's office is strictly judicial, and requires him to separate the fact on which he has to decide, from all the accidents that may have shaped it;—but the ordinary and irresponsible judgments of men are apt to measure merit in relation to the circumstances amid which it grew. The flower that has struggled into beauty under unfavourable conditions of air and light, testifies to more than common vigour in the soil whence it sprang:—and they whose sense has, first, been secured by the absolute claims of a work of art, are, for the most part, willing to add something to their admiration, on the score of any peculiar difficulties under which it may have been achieved.

This is a principle to which the Editor of these pages would not consent to appeal, on behalf of their Author, if it went the length of excusing the negative as well as enhancing the positive,—of imputing desert, instead of only acknowledging it with warmth:—but *they* are, in general, the most impatient under an appeal to their indulgence having no foundation in merit, who are most liberal in its grant where their sympathies have been bespoken by the language of genius. It is the Editor's wish, then, to put forward all these claims for Miss Brown;—to add the merit of her tale to the merit of her poetry,—taking them in that order—referring the reader to the poetry first, which speaks of her mind, and then asking him to turn to the tale that tells of her life. It is with the music in his ear of some of those beautiful little poems which occupy the miscellaneous portion of the volume, that the Editor would engage him in the touching account of those impeding circumstances amid which has welled up this fountain of natural song. The reader of that narrative will rather wonder that so little indulgence should be needed, than refuse the indulgence which is unhesitatingly asked.

The story of Miss Brown's mental education is well worth telling—both for its own interest and for its example. It is at once curious and instructive to watch a strong mind developing itself under conditions of social and physical disadvantage so great,—groping, by the aid of its poetic instincts, through the darkness of which it was conscious,—appropriating to itself everything whence it could draw nourishment, in the barren elements by which it was surrounded,—fastening upon all that could help it onward, while, by its own undirected energies, it was struggling upwards to the light. Excellent rules for self-training—the promptings of a clear natural intellect—may be deduced from the narrative; which is best related in the language of the poetess herself,—its humble incidents taking increased interest from the personality and simplicity of her narration.

"I was born," she says,—writing to a friend, whose communication of her letter has enabled the Editor to make Miss Brown her own biographer,—" on the 16th of January, 1816, at Stranorlar, a small village in the county Donegal. My father was then, and still continues to be, the postmaster of the village. I was the seventh child in a family of twelve; and my infancy was, I believe, as promising as that of most people: but, at the age of eighteen months, not having received the benefit of Jenner's discovery, I had the misfortune to lose my sight by the small pox, which was then prevalent in our neighbourhood. This, however, I do not remember,—and, indeed, recollect very little of my infant years. I never received any regular education,— but very early felt the want of it; and the first time I remember to have experienced this feeling strongly was about the beginning of my seventh year, when I heard our pastor (my parents being members of the Presbyterian church) preach for the first time. On the occasion alluded to, I was particularly struck by many words in the sermon, which, though in common use, I did not then understand; and from that time adopted a plan for

acquiring information on this subject. When a word
unintelligible to me happened to reach my ear, I was care-
ful to ask its meaning from any person whom I thought
likely to inform me—a habit which was, probably,
troublesome enough to the friends and acquaintances of
my childhood: but by this method I soon acquired a
considerable stock of words; and, when further advanced
in life, enlarged it still more by listening attentively to
my young brothers and sisters reading over the tasks
required at the village school. They were generally
obliged to commit to memory a certain portion of the
Dictionary and English Grammar, each day; and by
hearing them read it aloud frequently for that purpose,
as my memory was better than theirs (perhaps rendered
so by necessity), I learned the task much sooner than
they, and frequently heard them repeat it."

The whole of this narrative is, it will be seen, full of
useful morals and appeals to the sympathies of the right-
minded. It furnishes a striking example of the way in
which the absence of the gifts denied may be compen-
sated by a right use of the gifts that are left, and a
position of apparent barrenness compelled into the yield-
ing of abundance. For the acquisition of the intelligent
graces, no lot could well seem more hopeless than Miss
Brown's at the outset of her mental life, as stated in the
above simple paragraph. De Foe's castaway was not
more apparently helpless and companionless on his desert
island, than this young girl, cut off by her calamity from
the peopled world of vision, and left to an intellectual lone-

liness whose resources she had none to help her in finding
out. The hint given by the preaching of the pastor was
the first "foot-print left on the sand" of her desolate place,
by the native genius which she afterwards reclaimed
and made a friend of, and educated,—till it did her pre-
cious service, and pointed out to her all the fruitful places
of her solitude. It "showed her the best springs," and
"plucked her berries" in that seeming waste;—filling
it with occupations, and peopling it with friends, that
smiled upon her darkness, like the forms of the un-
known world which dawned upon the inexperience of
Miranda:—

> " How many goodly creatures are there here !
> . . . .   O brave new world,
> That has such people in't !"

But Miss Brown, as has been observed, tells her own
story best.

" My first acquaintance with books was necessarily
formed amongst those which are most common in country
villages. *Susan Gray—The Negro Servant—The
Gentle Shepherd—Mungo Park's Travels*—and, of
course, *Robinson Crusoe*—were among the first of my
literary friends; for I often heard them read by my
relatives, and remember to have taken a strange delight
in them when I am sure they were not half under-
stood. Books have been always scarce in our remote
neighbourhood,—and were much more so in my child-
hood: but the craving for knowledge which then com-
menced grew with my growth; and, as I had no books

of my own in those days, my only resource was borrowing from the few acquaintances I had,—to some of whom I owe obligations of the kind that will never be forgotten. In this way, I obtained the reading of many valuable works, though generally old ones;—but it was a great day for me when the first of Sir Walter Scott's works fell into my hands. It was *The Heart of Mid Lothian;* and was lent me by a friend, whose family were rather better provided with books than most in our neighbourhood.

" My delight in the work was very great, even then; and I contrived, by means of borrowing, to get acquainted, in a very short time, with the greater part of the works of its illustrious author,—for works of fiction, about this time, occupied all my thoughts. I had a curious mode of impressing on my memory what had been read—namely, lying awake, in the silence of the night, and repeating it all over to myself. To that habit I probably owe the extreme tenacity of memory which I now possess; but, like all other good things, it had its attendant evil,—for I have often thought it curious that, whilst I never forget any scrap of knowledge collected, however small, yet the common events of daily life slip from my memory so quickly that I can scarcely find anything again which I have once laid aside. But this misfortune has been useful, in teaching me habits of order."

The above is an interesting remark,—pointing out a distinction, the psychology of which does not, however,

seem far to seek. That sense by which the merely trivial
and inexpressive occurrences of the outer world make
their chief impression, had, in the case of the author,
been early closed against their passage to her memory.
Passing events on which the heart puts no stamp, the
eye must mark, or they run the risk of being lost amid
the lumber of the mind. But the knowledge for which
her spirit thirsted came in, by many of its natural
avenues, to a mind eager to appropriate and mark it at
once,—and memory, in the sound subject, registers all
that the heart receives. To a mind thus hungering, and
digesting in the dark, everything she heard that con-
tained in itself the nourishing principle, yielded literary
chyle, on which her intellectual constitution fed and
expanded; and the knowledge so acquired became an
indefeasible portion of her mental self. She had too
many visitors in her world of shadows, to take note
of all that came and went in the world of ordinary
things about her. In some respects, the blind bard may,
perhaps, be a gainer by the calamity which shuts out
the scene of common things, and turns the vision inward.
Milton had taken leave for ever of the faces of the earth,
ere he met the angels face to face in Paradise:—but *he*
was familiar with the commonplaces of the outer world,
long ere his darkness came down—was a man of business
and detail,—and the distinction which Miss Brown per-
ceives in the power of her own memory, as applied to
differing subjects, is the more easily explained *because*
it had no existence with him.

" About the beginning of my thirteenth year, I happened to hear a friend read a part of Baines's *History of the French War*. It made a singular impression on my mind; and works of fiction, from that time, began to lose their value, compared with the far more wonderful Romance of History. But books of the kind were so scarce in our neighbourhood, that Hume's *History of England*, and two or three other works on the same subject, were all I could reach,—till a kind friend, who was then the teacher of our village-school, obliged me with that voluminous work, *The Universal History*. There I heard, for the first time, the histories of Greece and Rome, and those of many other ancient nations. My friend had only the ancient part of the work; but it gave me a fund of information, which has been subsequently increased from many sources;—and at present I have a tolerable knowledge of History.

" My historical studies made a knowledge of Geography requisite;—but my first efforts to acquire it had been made even in childhood, by inquiring from every person the situation and locality of distant places which they chanced to mention. As I grew older, and could understand the language of books, the small abridgments of Geography, which were used by my brothers and sisters at the village school, were committed to memory, by a similar process to that by which I had learnt the Dictionary and Grammar. In order to acquire a more perfect knowledge of the relative situations of distant places, I sometimes requested a friend, who could trace maps, to place my finger upon some well-known spot, the situation of which I had exactly ascertained,—and then conduct the fingers of the other hand, from the points thus marked, to any place on the map whose position I wished to know,—at the same time mentioning the places through which my fingers passed. By this plan, having previously known how the cardinal points were placed, I was enabled to form a tolerably correct idea, not only of the boundaries and magnitude of various countries, but also of the courses of rivers and mountain-chains.

" The first geographical problem that I remember, occurred to me on hearing, in an account of the discovery of America, that Columbus at first intended to reach the coasts of Asia by sailing to the west; and, as I knew that Asia was in the eastern portion of the world, as laid down on our maps, the statement puzzled me much. At length, however, hearing our village teacher explain to my elder brothers and sisters the globular figure of the earth, that problem was solved;—but to comprehend it cost me the study of a sleepless night!

" As I increased in years and knowledge, the small school-books already mentioned were found insufficient; and I had recourse to my old method of borrowing. By this, I obtained some useful information; and increased it by conversation with the few well-informed persons who came within the limited sphere of my acquaintance. In the pursuit of knowledge, my path was always impeded by difficulties too minute and numerous to mention; but the want of sight was, of course, the principal one,—which, by depriving me of the power of reading, obliged me to depend on the services of others; and as the condition of my family was such as did not admit of much leisure, my invention was early taxed to gain time for those who could read. I sometimes did the work assigned to them, or rendered them other little services;—for, like most persons similarly placed, necessity and habit have made me more active in this respect than people in ordinary circumstances would suppose. The lighter kinds of reading were thus easily managed; but my young relatives were often unwilling to waste their breath and time with the drier, but more instructive, works which I latterly preferred. To tempt them to this, I used, by way of recompence, to relate to them long stories, and even novels, which perhaps they had formerly read but forgotten:—and thus my memory may be said to have earned supplies for itself.

"About the end of my fifteenth year, having heard much of the Iliad, I obtained the loan of Pope's translation. That was a great event to me; but the effect it produced requires some words of explanation. From my earliest years, I had a great and strange love of poetry; and could commit verses to memory with greater rapidity than most children. But at the close of my seventh year, when a few Psalms of the Scotch version, Watts's *Divine Songs*, and some old country songs (which certainly were not divine) formed the whole

of my poetical knowledge, I made my earliest attempt
in versification—upon that first and most sublime lesson
of childhood, *The Lord's Prayer*. As years increased,
my love of poetry, and taste for it, increased also, with
increasing knowledge. The provincial newspapers, at
times, supplied me with specimens from the works of
the best living authors. Though then unconscious of the
cause, I still remember the extraordinary delight which
those pieces gave me,—and have been astonished to find
that riper years have only confirmed the judgments of
childhood. When such pieces reached me, I never
rested till they were committed to memory; and after-
wards repeated them, for my own amusement, when
alone, or during those sleepless nights to which I have
been, all my life, subject. But a source of still greater
amusement was found in attempts at original composi-
tion; which, for the first few years, were but feeble
imitations of everything I knew—from the Psalms to
Gray's *Elegy*. When the poems of Burns fell in my
way, they took the place of all others in my fancy:—
and this brings me up to the time when I made my first
acquaintance with the *Iliad*.

"It was like the discovery of a new world, and effected
a total change in my ideas on the subject of poetry.
There was, at the time, a considerable manuscript of my
own productions in existence,—which, of course, I re-
garded with some partiality; but Homer had awakened
me,—and, in a fit of sovereign contempt, I committed
the whole to the flames. Soon after I had found the

b

Iliad, I borrowed a prose translation of Virgil,—there
being no poetical one to be found in our neighbourhood;
and in a similar manner made acquaintance with many
of the classic authors. But after Homer's, the work
that produced the greatest impression on my mind was
Byron's *Childe Harold.* The one had induced me to
burn my first manuscript,—and the other made me re-
solve against verse-making in future; for I was, then,
far enough advanced to know my own deficiency—but
without apparent means for the requisite improvement.
In this resolution I persevered for several years, and
occupied my mind solely in the pursuit of knowledge; but,
owing to adverse circumstances, my progress was neces-
sarily slow. Having, however, in the summer of the year
1840, heard a friend read the story of La Pérouse, it
struck me that there was a remarkable similarity be-
tween it and one related in an old country song, called
the *Lost Ship,* which I had heard in my childhood.
The song in question was of very low composition; but
there was one line at the termination of each verse
which haunted my imagination,—and I fancied might
deserve a better poem. This line, and the story of La
Pérouse, together with an irresistible inclination to
poetry, at length induced me to break the resolution I
had so long kept;—and the result was, the little poem
called *La Pérouse,* which will be found at page 207 of
this volume. Soon after, when Messrs. Gunn & Came-
ron commenced the publication of their *Irish Penny
Journal,* I was seized with a strange desire to contri-

bute something to its pages. My first contribution was favourably received; and I still feel grateful for the kindness and encouragement bestowed upon me by both the editor and the publishers. The three small pieces which I contributed to that work were the first of mine that ever appeared in print,—with the exception of one of my early productions which a friend had sent to a provincial paper. The *Irish Penny Journal* was abandoned, on the completion of the first volume: but the publishers, with great kindness, sent me one of the copies,—and this was the first book of any value that I could call my own! But the gift was still more esteemed as an encouragement—and the first of the kind.

" At this juncture, I had heard much of the London *Athenæum*; and the accounts of it which the provincial papers contained made me long to see it,—but no copies reached our remote neighbourhood. Finding it impossible to borrow the publication, I resolved to make a bold effort to obtain it; and in the spring of the year 1841, having a number of small poems on hand, I addressed them to the Editor, promised future contributions, and solicited that a copy of the journal might be sent to me as the return. My application was long unanswered; and I had given up all for lost,—when the arrival of many numbers of the journal, and a letter from the Editor, astonished me, and gratified a wish which had haunted my very dreams. From that period, my name and pretensions have been more before the public—many poems of mine having appeared in the pages of that publication, in Mr. Hood's *Magazine*, and in the *Keepsake* edited by the Countess of Blessington. Ten only of those contributed to the *Athenæum* have been included in the present collection—because most of them were so widely copied into the journals of the day, that I feared they might be too familiar for repetition. I have little more to tell;—this story of my mind's progress being the story of my life. My contributions to the *Athenæum*, and its Editor's kindness, shortly enabled me to procure some instructive books, which supplied in some measure the want of early education—while they have been, in my solitude, unspeakable sources of entertainment. I have few memories, to disturb my grateful recollection of those who have cheered me onward in my chosen but solitary path."

In the long letter from which these extracts are taken, there are other passages furnishing interesting examples of the earnestness which let no opportunity escape that might help to reverse the seeming decree of her destiny, by which the author was shut out from the tree of knowledge. Thus, an opportunity having come in her way for acquiring, through the kindness of a friend, a knowledge of the French language,—poetry, and some objects in connexion with it very dear to her imagination, are put resolutely aside, for the purpose of securing this one more golden bough. One of the first consequences derived by her, from the fact of her talent coming back to her in the shape of money, amid all the pride

and exhilaration of the circumstance, is the education of
a young sister, with a portion of that money, to be her
amanuensis. Every step gained by her in learning,
valued for itself, is valued more as the road to another.
The knowledge earned is at once invested in the purchase
of further knowledge. Of all the fruit which she
gathers the seed is saved for a new increase. The energy
displayed, from her childhood, by this almost friendless
girl, raises, the Editor cannot but think, at once the
interest and the character of her muse. There is some-
thing touching—and teaching, too,—in the picture of
that perseverance which has conquered for itself an inner
world of thought, in lieu of that outer world so early
withdrawn from the sense. The bard gathers dignity
from the darkness amid which she sings—as the dark-
ness itself is lightened by the song. There are lessons to
be drawn from both;—and the Editor believes that this
little volume has a variety of titles which should pro-
mise it a sure and extended popularity.

On the subject of the leading poem in the present
collection, Miss Brown must be heard for herself:—

"It was written," she says, "as all my other pieces have
been, neither by the advice of friends nor with the hope
of success,—but merely 'for the love of the thing,' if I
may use an expression very common in my country. It
has no better foundation than a newspaper story, which,
a few years ago, appeared in many of the British jour-
nals, and was said to have been copied from a Russian
paper:—but it took a strong hold on my mind, at the

time; and nothing but the want of information pre-
vented me from attempting the subject long ago. For
any errors and mistakes I can only plead that the land
is new to me—and comparatively little known, I
believe, to all."

Had Miss Brown decided, in consultation with friends,
it is probable that, for these reasons, and some others
existing in the subject itself, they might have warned
her off this particular ground:—but she who has done so
much for, and by, herself, may, it is submitted, hope for
some allowance and consideration on the part of those
who prefer her lyrics to her lengthened poem.

THE STAR OF ATTÉGHÉI.

THE STAR OF ATTÉGHÉI:

A TALE OF CIRCASSIA.

———

Muse of my country! thou hast sung
Of many sorrows; yet thy lyre
Is sweet, as when by Ossian strung,
To breathe of love or freedom's fire.
Though stranger feet have trodden down
Both Tara's towers and Brian's crown,—
Yet still, through all her blighted springs,
The ancient harp of Erin rings,
With numbers mighty as, of old,
O'er battle-field and banquet rolled,
When rose upon the western clime
The glory of its early prime.

For thine the bard whose lyre hath slept,—
But slept beneath his laurels' shade,
That early caught, and long have kept
A living verdure, ne'er to fade,—
The greenness of his native hills,—
Whose wildest waste his music fills,

B

Or journies, with thy children, far
As shines the morn or evening star;
For oft his sweet inspiring strains
Awake Columbia's western plains,
Or reach the eastward wanderer's ear,
Beside the rose-crowned Bendemere.

Muse of my country! if thy smile
May beam on tuneless harps like mine—
As o'er our darkest homes, the while,
Some gleams of early glory shine—
I ask not for the bays that shed
Their greenness o'er thy glorious dead:
Their grace is for a nobler brow;—
But breathe upon my spirit, now,
The freshness of the garland worn
By him, thy last and brightest-born,
When first he struck his harp, to sing
The lay of Tara's breaking string!
For mine is but a broken chord;
And if it breathe of distant lands,
It is that Erin's fame is poured
In loftier strains, by mightier hands:
A thousand bards have sung the shore,—
But none have ever loved it more.
Though not to souls like mine belong
The glorious heritage of song,
Yet, if my hand have power to wake

The theme which mightier bards forsake,
Muse of my country's song, inspire
At once the minstrel and the lyre!

    *   *   *   *

   My lay is of a land unknown
To Europe's minstrelsy,—though strown
With wrecks and relics of her fame,[1]
And bright with many an early dream
Of far but unforgotten ages:
And since the last of Ilion's line[2]—
The sons of warriors, bards and sages—
Are left to such a lyre as mine,
I would the song, though sad, should be
Of glory, love and liberty!

   For glorious is the mountain land
That rises o'er the Euxine Sea,—
With towering cliffs so wildly grand,
And forests waving wide and free,
O'er ruined tower and rocky steep,
And lovely valley green and deep;—
Where, far amid the boundless blue,
The mighty mountains close the view,
In misty majesty, with zone
Of cloud and glacier, dimly lone,—
The eagle's rest—the tempest's throne!
Or, robed in all the gorgeous dyes
That only shine from eastern skies,

They might have claimed the brightest page
Of Harold's glorious pilgrimage,—
By yet more azure heavens o'erhung,
And loftier than the Alps he sung!

Oh! many a winter's gift of snow
Hath fallen upon her mountain's head,
And many a summer's glorious glow
From Aboun's flowery banks hath fled,[3]
And many a shrine hath been profaned,
And turf and torrent darkly stained,
And many a heart and home laid low,
Or desolate with early woe,
Since first the dusky eagle turned
On Attéghéi his greedy gaze,[4]—
When Persia for her Shiraz mourned,
And Othman trembled at the blaze
Of Gothic glory, that surrounded
The Northern Idol—so compounded
Of clay and iron as to seem
The feet of Nebonassar's dream!
And must the iron fall on thee,
Now, in the day-spring of thy soul,
Mother of Asia's chivalry!
O! for the prophet's power to roll
The locust billows back once more
Upon their bleak and barren shore,
And give the early verdure back

To all their battle-blasted track!
For wide their wasteful pinions spread
O'er fallen nations;—Poland's lance
Was shivered, and her bravest bled,
In vain:—may other, happier chance
Await thy starry banner! once[5]
The cross waived o'er thee;—from the steep
Of Elbrûz, yet, it tells thy sons
Where low the last Crusaders sleep;[6]
And now, the same bright banner leads
Thy spoiler to his darkest deeds!

But Caucasus still rises round thee,
With all his wealth of wood and wave;
And still, as when Iskander found thee,
Thy maids are bright, thy warriors brave,—
Brave as when, from their mountain brows,
They smote the pride of Tartar bows,[7]
Bright as their swords have ever been
Among the Moslem legions seen,
When leading on their breaking ranks
Against the thunder-bearing Franks,
By Nilus' or by Danube's banks.
Ah! noble service, ill repaid!
Why wakes not now each warrior's shade,
To curse the base and thankless throne,
That left thee in the storm alone,
And gave thee, as thy valour's meed,

Desertion in the hour of need?
Woe, for the nations that have given
Their glory to the stranger!—ne'er
Shall earth repay that precious leaven:
The poet's song, the patriot's spear,
May wake, on many a distant shore,
The soul of freedom, never more
To sleep, and twine their country's name
With many a deed of deathless fame;
But who shall gather from the grave,
In Syria's waste or Tigris' wave,
Circassia's early-perished brave?—
Who shall reclaim, from Europe's fields,
Sarmatia's bright but broken shields,—
Or give *my* country back the hearts
That led the world in arms and arts?
Ah! such hath ever been *her* lot,
The faithful but the still forgot!

How glorious were the steps of Greece,
Among her laurels, long ago,
At Marathon and Salamis!
But never, in the brightest glow
Of all her fame,—though treasured long
In storied page or poet's song,—
Were found more bravely wielded brands,
More fearless hearts and faithful hands,
Than those who followed where the sheen

Of Sangiac-Sheriff, starry green,
Led on through many a bloody scene,—
From where the Kouban's fatal swamp
Protects the hated Cossack's camp,
To where the early sunlight falls
On far Pitzounda's lonely walls!*

Brave were the warriors, high their fame,
As sung amid their native land;—
But there were two, who early came
To princely Guzbeg's gallant band,
Two stranger chiefs, whom they who met,
In peace or war, could ne'er forget.
Young were they both, and wondrous fair,—
And yet some early touch of care
Had left upon each youthful face
A strange and an untimely trace.
The one was of a foreign race;
But if his eagle glance had less
Of fierceness than the dark Tcherkesse,
It beamed a soul to theirs allied
In patriot zeal and martial pride,—
Though far in Christian climes, I ween,
The country of his birth had been.
The other, he was fairer far,
And seemed of true Circassian race,—
Yet moved among them like a star
That early left its ancient place,

And might return no more,—but ne'er
Forgot that bright, forsaken sphere;
And, from the spirit proud and high
That lighted up his glorious eye,
They called him "Star of Attéghéi."
Yet, sooth, that stranger's form and face
Seemed less for war than woman's gráce,—
But round him hung some hidden spell
That made the Adighé* love him well.

O! mighty was the soul that wrought
Such deeds, by such a fragile form,—
And soft the eye, at times, that caught
A lightning like the mountain storm,
When, as the forest in the blaze,
The Moscov withered in its gaze.
And still, by mountain gorge or glen,
Where fought or fell the shepherd men,
Where'er, along that leaguered coast,
A field was won, a fortress lost,
His spear was brightest in the host;
His step was foremost in the charge,—
And well he wielded sword or targe,—
Where'er the cannon's fiery breath
By thousands did the work of death,—
Yet spared a heart, so strangely brave
It seemed to look but to the grave.
And *him* the other followed still,

To guide and guard, through storm and strife,
As if his all of good or ill
Hung on that warrior's death or life.
Oft, in the battle's red career,
A shade of deep and deadly fear,
Swift as an arrow from the bow,
Would pass across that stranger's brow;
And well the watchful warriors guessed
Not for himself such terrors pressed
Upon the Polack's faithful breast.

O! lovely are the mountain maids,
With starry eyes and gleaming hair,
That shine among their native shades
The fairest even of Asia's fair:—
Alas! that e'er those free-born flowers
Should bloom for Othman's slavish bowers!
But clouds like this shall pass away,
As breaks their country's brighter day;
For well the mountain minstrel knows
The sweetness of his Alpine rose,—
And oft against his country's foes
The warrior bears a braver part
To win some patriot-maiden's heart.—
Yet sigh nor smile had power to charm
That youthful pair;—though many a glance
That even the heart of Age might warm
Was theirs, in festive bower or dance.—

For since Thalestris' heart was won
By the far fame of him that shone
The first and last of Macedon,
Circassia's gentler daughters own
The ancient power that ever gave
The heart of beauty to the brave!
But beauty, in its brightest bloom,
Unheeded met these stranger eyes:—
Perchance no other love had room
In hearts so bound by friendship's ties,
Or by the secret sorrow shared
Between themselves,—for none had heard
The hidden story of their past,
And they were strangers, to the last.

*   *   *   *

Onward the fleeting seasons flew;
And deadlier still the conflict grew,
That left, in spite of summer's dew
Or winter's all effacing flood,
Its story written deep in blood.
But still, the Moscov poured his hordes
In vain upon the mountain swords,—
For many a waste and many a grave
His legions found—but not a slave!

'Twas morn! On Kaff-Dagh's [19] glaciers vast
The rising sun his splendour cast,

And kindled, as with hand of flame,
The Kouban's old majestic stream;
That answered to her sister floods,
Far flashing through the dark green woods,
In their unfallen glory still
Enrobing many a matchless hill,
Whose towering peaks of stainless snow
Were beacons to the vales below:—
For there the earliest light was flung,
And there the latest glory hung;
The stars behind their heights retired,—
The setting sun their summits fired,—
And well might such bright summits be
The last strongholds of liberty!
But lately, 'mid that tranquil scene
The din of hostile arms had been,
When burst from grove and green recess
The children of the fair Tcherkesse,
To drive the Moscov legions far
Before the mountain scimitar:—
To-day, no sound of strife was there,
No trace of life in earth or air,
Save where the fading watchfire shone
From craggy summit, high and lone,
As fitfully its radiance fell
Upon the mountain sentinel,—
Who, armed in gleaming panoply,[11]
Stood forth against the morning sky,

Like some old knightly statue, left
Since the last Templar's helm was cleft!

But when the parting mists of night
Rolled upwards to the distant height,
From Aboun's valley rich and fair,
A clang of trumpets shook the air,—
Calling to solemn council there
Princes and people, scattered wide,
O'er distant vale and mountain side:
And lofty peak and cave profound,
In thunder echoed back the sound,—
Till high 'mid Anapa's turrets gray
Its lonely echoes died away.
And, as that mighty summons rose
O'er waving woods and gleaming snows,
From hidden depths of forest shade,
From dewy glen and tangled glade,
From cliffs where pealing torrents rang,
The mountain tribes by thousands sprang.
With shining arms, and tameless steed
Of matchless form and eagle speed,
With haughty glance and bearing high,
On sweeps the son of Attéghéi!
But never yet did Eastern queen
Ride forth with more imperial mien
Than came the daughters of the land,
In many a gay and graceful band;—

Whose raven locks and snowy veils,
Wide floating on the mountain gales,
Might tell of earth's unsullied years,
Ere woman's path grew dim with fears.
But, ah! the jewelled poniard told
Of darker days—of war that rolled
His bloody billows on their shore,
To blight the fairest flowers it bore!
The echoes of the fatal fields
That thinned their country's bravest shields,
Among the mountain maids awoke
The fires that slumbered, since the stroke
Of fate had withered from their clime
The sovereigns of its early time—
Whose fame through far tradition runs,
The long remembered Amazons.

     *   *   *   *

"Land of the lovely and the brave,—
Of Othman's conqueror and his slave!
Was it the mountain's breath that gave
Thy children, for their deathless dower,
Beauty and valour that outlast
The wreck of fame, the fall of power,
And all the shadowy glories cast
Upon the morning mists of time,—
The wandering meteors of the past,

The mirage of the mountain clime?
That filled the early dreams of Greece
With promise of the golden fleece;[12]
And lured to Asia's distant seas
The far adventuring Genoese?
Bright land, whose early beauty beams
Upon the eastern poet's dreams,—
From India's ever sacred streams,
To where the glow of Europe's morn
Upon the waning crescent gleams,
And lights up Stamboul's golden horn,—
But shines on none like thee and thine!
Bright mother of a matchless race,
That seem the last of Adam's line,—
In whom the wanderer's eye may trace
The early glory, left to tell
This withered world how far it fell!"—

Thus spake a wandering child of song,[13]
Who gazed upon that gathering throng,—
From where a lone and lofty tomb
Arose, beneath the verdant gloom
Of ancient oak and yew, that crowned
The summit of that mighty mound,—
Perchance a warrior's resting-place,
But raised by a forgotten race.[14]
Strange that, when tears and dust of ages
Have blotted out, from history's pages,

The names of nations past away,
Before the dawn of Egypt's day,—
Surviving palaces and fanes,
The earthy Pyramid remains,—
And the last record left, to save
From mute oblivion—is the grave!

There stood the bard,—but stood alone,
Like one among the tribes unknown:
And yet, the graceful garb he wore
Seemed of Abasia's rocky shore;
And in his eye there shone the fire
That well might wake the mountain lyre,
Which now he bore in silence, hung
Beside the gleaming sword it sung.
Though youth had left him, and his brow
Was marked with early furrows now,—
Which might have been but lines of thought,
By time to deeper channels wrought,—
Yet never seemed a minstrel's hand
More fit to wield the deadly brand,
In mountain-pass or forest fray,
Than his who lingered there, that day.

And bright, beyond a poet's praise,
The valley spread beneath his gaze:
Where fruitful fields of golden corn
Were bending to the breeze of morn;

And lovely was the dewy green
Of sunny slopes that lay between,—
Amid whose greenness breathed such flowers
As might have bloomed in Eden's bowers.
Yet lovelier far the hills around;
With bleating flocks and vineyards crowned,—
And stately groves of giant oak,
Beneath whose shadow curled the smoke
Of hidden homes, and foliage-shrined
From spoiler's eye and mountain wind:[15]—
For, since the early Druids prayed,
Or wild birds warbled in the shade,
The tangled wild and woodland brake
Have been the fortress of the weak;—
And love and freedom ever rest
Most safely by the wood-dove's nest!
But where the hills retired, and wide
The valley spread her verdant pride,
As if to form a battle-plain,
Where Liberty might count her slain,
At close of some victorious day,
Demirghoi's tents before him lay.[16]

Oh! simple dwellings,—earliest known,—
Ere yet the tyrant's tower of stone
Shut out the blessed sun and stars,
With dungeon-keep and prison bars!
Ye were, before the cities grew,

And have survived their glory too:—
For still ye rise along the shore
Where Babylon is found no more;
And still, as in the ancient years,
Are the best rampart freedom rears.
And braver bulwark never rose
Against a land's unsparing foes
Than those fair tents, so fitly spread
Where Aboun's silvery current sped,
Amid the valley's bosom green,—
Reflecting far the martial sheen
Of shining spears and gleaming mail,
That swept along that lovely vale:—
For there, since morning's planet set,
Had twice ten thousand warriors met.

The rush is o'er, the tents are still;
And now, beneath the sacred shade
Of trees no time had power to kill—
The ancient but the undecayed—
Where oft their fathers sat, of yore,
The mountain people met once more,—
With eyes as bright and hearts as brave
As ever saw above them wave
The giant branches, that might breathe
The story of their mountain land;—
For many a council met beneath,—
And many a warrior's votive brand

c

Among their sombre foliage hung,
And oft the minstrel's lay was sung
Beneath their shadows green and hoary,—
The tale of long departed glory.
Around them lay their famous dead;
And bright, o'er river, tent and tree,
With morning's sunlight o'er it shed,
Their starry standard floated free:—
An offering worthy of the queen,"
Whose memory kept the glorious green
That never leaves her native bowers,—
And sent, from Stamboul's regal towers,
To the bright valleys of her youth,
That token of her changeless truth,—
To bind in holy brotherhood
The sons of many a deadly feud.
Oh! when its princely bearer first
Unfurled that banner to the breeze,
What gladness swelled the shouts that burst
Beneath those old immortal trees!—
When rock and field and forest rang
Responsive to the brazen clang
Of clashing spears,—the sound that told
The Spartan warrior's joy, of old!
The mountains knew their children's voice,
That made their very snows rejoice,
And their old slumbering genii start—
The cry was from a nation's heart!

Like to some dark descending cloud,
Whose breast the summer lightning fills,
Were gathered in that earnest crowd
The strength and beauty of the hills:—
For aged sire and virgin fair
And child and warrior—all were there.
And there,—though none his country knew,—
That lonely minstrel mingled too,
With sons of many a distant shore,
That now had hopes and homes no more!
For Moscov power and Moscov hate
Had made their dwellings desolate,
And swords like theirs can best repay
The terrors of a tyrant's sway.
And there the homeless Tartar stood,—
Whose heart was in the desert still,
As when he saw the multitude
Of Timour's tents its silence fill,
And heard, through the eternal sands,
The march of Zinga's countless bands;—
There came the sons of Turcomain,—
The fair-browed Georgian,—and the swain
Of bright Mingrelia's fruitful plain:—
And, best and bravest of the throng,
The Pole, scarce deemed a stranger there,—
For, oft, his distant country's song
Arose upon the mountain air;
The strains that cheered his land, ere, yet,

She saw her star of freedom set,
And its last ray of hope depart,
Had found an echo in the heart
Of these old hills.—Oh! that the winds,
From their far heights, might waft again
That echo to the lonely pines
That bend o'er Praga's fatal plain,
Or Vistula's ensanguined flood,—
To tell the land that all her blood
Was not yet unavenged, nor all
Her glory fallen in Warsaw's wall!

Muse! mighty Muse! thy voice is still
For freedom; and to all the earth,
Far as the sun and stars fulfil
Their ceaseless course, it hath gone forth!
Where'er the steps of man have been,
Where hearths are bright or graves are green,
The glory of thy steps is seen,
Though dimly—as the Seer who trod
The steeps of Sinai, saw his God!
And still, where sleeps the stainless snow
On lofty Mkinvari's [18] rocky height,
Thy presence sheds the starry glow
That woke, in its immortal might,
The harp of Homer, when his theme
Was Ilion's fate and Hector's fall.
For heroes to this council came,

Who to the minstrel might recal
The flower of Ilion's proudest spears,—
But that a nobler cause inspired
These patriot chiefs, than ever fired
The warriors of the elder years
And ancient feuds—though never sung
As was the race whence these are sprung!

There sat Demirghoi's prince;—though brief
And calm his speech, and mild his mien,
Than Djamboulet a nobler chief
In camp or council ne'er had been,—
Since his lamented sire;[19] who bore
That more than royal name, before,
And perished in his glorious prime,
When thousands found a bloodless grave—
The only boon that Othman gave
The warriors of the mountain clime,
Save the sad lesson, truly taught
To all that have for freedom fought,
That, in their own unaided strength,
Their surest safety lies, at length.
But ah! how lonely sat the chief
Of Nottakhaitzi's lordly line,—
Aged, but stately as a pine
That storms had left without a leaf!
For pestilence had early made
His home a desert-place, and laid

Its roses in the dust; and they
Who fought and conquered by his side,
Had, one by one, in battle died,
And left him, in his later day,
Only the glorious hills for which
All else was given that made him rich.

There sat the youthful Islam, too,
Prince of the brave Khapsoukhie.   Say,
What passing cloud its shadow threw
Upon thy bride's young brow, that day,
As her sad gaze a moment fell
Upon the face she loved so well?
Was it a shade of coming fate
That darkened o'er her spirit then,—
A vision of that gory glen
In whose dark bosom, as relate
Her country's bards,[20] the early grave
Closed o'er the beautiful and brave?
And there, all restless, roved the glance
Of Hassan's dark and jealous eye,—
The last of Mamelukes whose lance
Flashed under Egypt's burning sky,
And smote the Arab spear and bow,—
He led the tameless Lesghi now:—
But, since the hour when Hassan fled
From Cairo's walls, the only guest
That left, alive, the deadly feast,[21]

Though brave in battle, it was said
He trusted nothing, but the steed
That bore him with such saving speed.

   Close by the jealous warrior's side,
There sat a chief of loftier fame
And nobler bearing; far and wide
Was known the gallant Gusbeg's name,—
The Cœur-de-Lion of the East,—
A prince alike in field and feast.
Though time had tinged his flowing beard,
And oft, perchance, in lonely hours,
When life deplores its trampled flowers,
The boy his anger might have spared[22]
Upon the father's heart would rise,
Like Agamemnon's sacrifice,—
Yet braver never wore the red,[23]
Nor in his country's battles bled.
And, with the leaders of the land
Who in that proud assembly met,
Sat Nirsis, leaning on his brand,
Which oft the dews of war had wet:
Upon that stern old Tartar's brow,
Scarred as it was, the eye might trace
The last of Zinga's royal race—
And best perchance—though throneless now,
And homeless too; for though his spear
Had served the Adighé many a year,

Yet these were not the trees that bent
In greenness o'er his father's tent.

But who is he that comes, at last,
With eye so bright and face so fair,
Yet sad, as though some blight had passed
Across the hope that once was there,
And dimmed its joy—but could not hide
Its beauty or its princely pride?
Few are his years and slight his frame,
And serf or vassal he has none,—
Nor friend to share his path but one;—
But the far hills have heard his fame:
And from that mighty multitude,
From royal Pshe and Tartar rude,
Breaks forth one wild tumultuous cry,—
"The Star—the Star of Attéghéi!"

Loud were the welcome and the joy—
A shout like that which hailed, before,
Their mountain banner; for the boy
Had won the laurels which he wore,—
And, though a stranger, took his place
Among the noblest of the race.
But there was one, whose weary eye
Had scanned the crowd, as if it sought
Some face that love had ne'er forgot,—
And saw the warrior chiefs pass by,

Alike unmoved by love or fear:
Yet, when that stranger-youth drew near,
At once the minstrel's gaze was fixed
On him; and o'er his brow there passed
A sudden gleam of gladness, mixed
With wonder,—for it seemed, at last,
His lost was found,—but found where he
Had never dreamt that face to see.

The princes sat in deep debate;
For on the councils of that day,
As in a balance, hung the fate
Of the unconquered Attéghéi.
The wiles of art, the powers of war,
All vainly tried, the baffled Czar
Had bid his bootless thunders cease;
And, o'er the hills, with words of peace,
Had come a princely messenger,—
The scion of as proud a tree
As ever sprang where Liberty
Was not—in northern pomp to bear
The olive-branch:—but ah! not now
Untaxed, as was the dove-borne bough,
So welcome to the weary eyes
Of the Old World's first mariner!
Its price was freedom:—such a price
The mountain people could not spare,
For that had cost their bravest blood,

By plague and famine, field and flood.
The herald came, with plume and banner;
And, though his train was wondrous small,
Sure in the old rude mountain honour
The Moscov feared nor sword nor thrall:
Full well those warrior-chiefs he knew;
For he had met them oft, before,
In peaceful hall and battle, too,—
And left upon the Euxine shore,
What few, of all the northern host,
In that unequal war, could boast,
A name undimmed and sword unstained
By aught that chivalry disdained.

He was a Boyar of noble strain,
And in the summer of his years,—
Though wanting in the fiery vein
And beauty of the mountaineers:
His pleasant eye and graceful mien
Seemed fitting for a courtly scene,
And his light tresses' golden glow
Told of the land of serfs and snow.
Bold was his speech and frankly spoken,
But yet persuasive, as the word
Of peace should be; and in unbroken
Silence, the gathered warriors heard.
But when, at length, the hated name
Of *subject* smote their startled ears,

At once, like some resistless flame,
The flash of twice ten thousand spears,
Full in the herald's startled sight,
Gleamed o er the valley far and bright!

And thus the gallant Gusbeg spoke:—
"Moscov! thou hast our answer, now!
For while our country's sword and bow
Can send a dart or lend a stroke,
Its children bear no foreign yoke!"
He paused—for on the winds arose
Their loud defiance; till it woke
The echoes of the ancient snows,—
And the old glaciers, in their glee,
Caught up that voice of Liberty!

But when the burst was o'er, the chief
Of the dark Tartars rose, and bent
Upon the Boyar his eye, where grief—
The pang of many years—seemed blent
With the still quenchless thirst that clings
To the heart's deserts, when the springs
Of hope are dried, and love is sought
No more,—and there remaineth nought
Save vengeance for its only thought.
So looked the Tartar, as he said:—
"Moscov! where are the nations gone
With whom, of old, your fathers made

Such peace?   They dwelt beneath the shade
Of Kouban's woods; the woods wave on,
Still green and glorious, to the day,
And the great river wends its way
To the wide sea—but where are they?
Where sleeps the Ossetinian bow?
The Georgian spear,—of old so bright?
And where my own high people now,
The firm in faith—the famed in fight?
Where are my father's tent and throne?
Where are the warrior-chiefs that shone
Around me?—for I am alone!
Thou answerest not! the iron hoof
Of tyranny hath trodden down
The arm of might—the heart of proof:
And must the haughty despot's frown
Fall on these wild, free mountains, too?
No! children of the hills, for you
Are better hopes!   The western thrones
Are mighty—mightiest hers, the queen
Whose sceptered rule the ocean owns:
The farthest Indian shores have seen
Her banner; and the utmost isle
That sees the dying sunset smile
Beholds her ever wandering sails;—
The Moscovite before them quails!—
And there, perchance, some sword may wake,
If not for yours, for freedom's sake?"

He ceased:—and 'mong the chiefs arose
The youthful stranger; but he gazed
Not on the people's burning brows,
Nor where his country's banner blazed:—
For, even then, his eye was raised
Where the far mountains, in the power
Of their untrodden majesty,
Arose, like children of the sky;—
They were his country's changeless dower,
The pride and bulwark of her shore,
And he had loved them, evermore!
And thus he spoke:—" O warriors, trust
Not in cold Europe! she stood by,
Till Poland's hope was in the dust,—
And heard the long and sleepless cry
Of trampled Greece, and could forget,
Through years of blood and hopeless ages,
The still unpaid, uncounted debt
She owed the land, whose priceless pages
Had lit her children's path to fame;
And, when her tardy succours came,
They gave—*not* freedom, but the name!
An empty name!—So might it be—
E'en so, my glorious land, with thee!

" Was it for this thy valour turned
The Grecian, ere his course was done,
And from thy mountain fastness spurned

The conqueror marching to the sun?—
From old Olympus' sacred height,
To Indus' darkly-rolling wave,
Thine was the only sword to smite
His iron host:—how long the grave
Hath closed above his power; whilst thou
Art tameless—as he left thee—now!
Was it for this thy children barred
The passage to their mountain home,
Against the last of Greeks,[24] who dared
The terrors of almighty Rome?
Rome's gift of empire Time hath reft,—
Thy gift was freedom—*that* is left!
Yes, mine own country! though thy rills
Run red, through valleys once so fair,
There has been freedom on our hills
Since Zoroaster[25] worshipped there—
And they shall own, till time be done,
No other sovereign than the Sun!

" Our brave have perished; and our young
Have fallen, as fall the summer flowers
Before the scythe; for we have flung
On freedom's altar, all of ours
That Time could give, or take,—and more,
Perchance, than time can e'er restore,—
Our first affections—in the bloom
Of life and hope that early fell,—

And we have seen the fire consume
The costly sacrifice:—'tis well!
It was accepted; 'mid our woes,
Though homes are dark and hearths are chill,
Brothers! we have the stainless snows
And the unchanging mountains, still!"

Up rose the princes,—and up rose
The people; for the die was cast,
That hour!   But ere their wild applause
And the loud clang of spears were past,
The jealous Hassan spoke, at last.
For long, upon the stranger bard,
The chief had fixed his stern regard;—
And, if an eye had power to blast
The hope of life, it was the look
Of that dark, jealous Mameluke.
The minstrel saw it not: it seemed
His thoughts were of the youth, whose speech
The warriors reverenced,—for they deemed
Him strangely wise; nor sage nor leech
His depth of knowledge e'er could reach,—
And oft the aged chiefs would say
That he had learned the mystic lore
By eastern magi taught, of yore—
The wisdom of an elder day.
For still his words had power to sway
The councils of the mountain peers,

Where swords were bright and beards were gray:—
Smooth were his cheeks and green his years;
Yet even o'er Hassan's iron soul
He held a high and strange control.

But sternly spoke the Lesghian, then,
As prince and peasant lingered still:—
" Well may the Moscov forge a chain
For us and ours; his craft and skill
Alike our camps and councils fill
With hidden spies.—Strange minstrel, say,
Whence comest thou—and why alone?[26]
And give thy tale, at least, the tone
Of truth;—for I have marked, to-day,
Thy searching gaze, which seemed to me
More crafty than a bard's should be!"

" Chiefs of the Attéghéi"! replied
The minstrel,—gazing, calmly cold,
Upon the serfs, on every side,
Who thronged around him,—" ye behold,
In me, no traitor; though my glance
Hath more of curious search, perchance,
Than well befits a son of song.
But I have been a searcher, long:—
O'er peopled vale and mountain wild,
Through battle-field and festive throng,
Even as a father for his child,

So have I sought, in vain, for one,
The fairest-born beneath the sun.
And if the warriors deign to hear
My tale, though more of love than fear,
It might beguile a warrior's ear."

   " My days of love have seen their last,"—
Said gallant Gusbeg; " yet my heart
Grows green, in memory of the past:—
And, minstrel, if thy tale impart
The poet's potent charm, to bring
The freshness of their early spring
To withered hearts—or teach our youth
The power of love's unchanging truth,
Our time were well bestowed, in sooth.
And, for thy safety, on my sword,
I pledge thee here a warrior's word,—
For ne'er did prying Moscov wear
Such stately form and martial air."

   The chiefs in fixed attention set,
The peasants round the minstrel pressed:
For, there, the Muse is mighty yet,—
As, in the nations of the west,
Her power hath been, when Runic song"
Redeemed a monarch's deadly wrong.
And even the parting Moscov stayed
His steed, to hear the minstrel's tale;

D

And Hassan's eye no more surveyed
The valley paths; and many a veil
Upon the winds unheeded flew,—
For ever dear to woman's heart
Hath been the minstrel's sacred art;
And listening maidens nearer drew,—
As thus, amid the glittering van
Of warrior men, the bard began.

  *   *   *   *

 " Know ye Pitzounda's lovely bay,
That 'mid its circling mountains lies,
Where cedar-forests stretch away,
From the bright waters to the skies;
Till in the distant azure fades
The glory of the sylvan shades?
Though seeming ever young and vernal,
And, in their ancient growth, eternal,
Yet, through their depths of pathless green
The Moscov's wasteful axe hath been;
And, now, a fortress' walls are seen
Amid the leafy solitude,
Where once a Grecian city stood.
But time hath left no wreck, to tell
How that proud city rose or fell,—
Save one unfallen fane, whose spire
Reflects the sunset's fading fire,
And stands, a refuge, in the path
Of him who flees from human wrath.

" There is another fortress, there,
Though nearer to the mountain's breast;
Yet fruitful fields and vineyards fair
Surround it,—for the spot was blest
By some far wandering saint, they say,
Who rested there upon his way.
Of old, the Zazi-oku band
Were robbers of their native land,—
And bore away inglorious spoil,
Won from the children of the soil ;
But, now, the years of strife are o'er,—
The Zazi-oku spoil no more.
Yet, still, upon the mountain cliff,
Arise the old and stately towers,
The dwelling of their princely chief,—
But built by other hands than ours:
A relic of those iron men[28]
Who raised, of old, by wave and glen,
Their towers,—that, like the living rock,
Defied the sword and tempest-shock,
And cost our country years of woe
And war, before she laid them low :—
So ever perish freedom's foe!
But one was spared,—whose stately dome
Pitzounda's princes made their home;
And oft, beneath the battlement,
From which the dark invader sent

His Red-cross banner forth, of yore,
Some dreams of feudal power came o'er
These eastern chiefs, that less became
Their country than their castle's fame.

  "And he who holds that fortress old
Is no less lordly than his sires
In other days; but low and cold
In him have grown their martial fires:—
For he has laid the sword aside,
And bowed to Moscov power and pride.
I know not if it were to gain
The sway his fathers sought in vain,
Of yore,—or for some baser bribe,
He sold the freedom of his tribe:
But, whether bought by power or gold,
That heritage was cheaply sold.
Yet, many a vassal owneth he,—
For Zaphor is a noble Pshe,
And by the mountain tribes revered,
But ever trusted less than feared
Among his northern friends;—so, still,
The evil doers dream of ill!

  "His youth in mountain war was spent;—
But he hath past his manhood's prime,
And long forsaken field and tent:
Far better, now, he loves the chime

Of choral voices, ringing free,
Around the old and sacred tree,—
When Merem's ancient feast is spread,[20]
And harvest moons their splendour shed
On fading woods and golden fields,
Whose glory to the sickle yields,—
Than martial trump or charging cheer,
That tell of death or glory near
To the young warrior's heart and ear.
The trumpets have no power to wake
The frozen heart, that could forsake
His country, in her trying hour,
And kneel to her invader's power.
And such is Zaphor:—yet his home
Is happy; pestilence or sword
Hath not been there,—and brightly bloom
His children round the hearth and board.
For, though the thunder called to rest
His first-beloved—perchance his best—
Yet he hath now a second bride,
Who smiles, with all a mother's pride,
On boys as brave and girls as fair
As ever claimed a father's care.
But, ah! the loveliest maiden, there,
Was one, upon whose blooming years
There fell no mother's smiles or tears!
Her childhood saw the wild flowers bloom
Upon that mother's early tomb,—

Who left her but her lonely part
Among the tribes—a stranger's heart!

" For she had been a stranger,—born
Where the far vineyards of the west
Are blushing, bright as summer's morn
On lofty Mkinvera's snow-white crest.
Hers was the fair and pleasant land—
The known and loved on every strand—
To which the warrior, bard and sage
Have left a glorious heritage
Of thought, that owns no conqueror's thrall,
And fame, that cannot fade or fall
With sceptre or with city wall.
Never, on Europe's chequered story,
Were shed such gleams of hope and glory,
Since on the Grecian summits, first,
The day-spring of the nations burst,
As those that lit her country's march
From Danube's wave to Titus' arch:—
And yet, the star of those bright years
Arose in blood, and set in tears!

" How stately was the host whose might
It led against our country's foes:
But—how hath glory turned to night!—
They sleep beneath the northern snows!
And she, that maiden's mother, shared

Her country's hopes; and early dared
The perils of the northern war,—
For love had lured her footsteps, far
From home and kindred:—but the grave
Closed o'er her early bright and brave,
And she became a Cossack's slave.
Long years ago, when Zaphor led
A chosen band, where darkly spread
Tchernemorsky's tents,—the cravens fled,
With all their wealth; nor serf nor spoil
Repaid the Zazi-oku's toil.
But, by the Kouban's sedgy bound,
That fairer prize the warriors found;—
Yet sad and worn she seemed, as one
From whom the hope of life was gone.

" But Zaphor was a mountain chief:
He bore her to his mother's home,—
Where love and friendship soothed her grief,
And bade her friendless footsteps roam
No more; for to his household hearth
She found a stronger tie than birth,
When Zaphor wooed, as chief should woo,
And won the gentle stranger too.
And many a mountain chief, beside,
Had vainly sought her for his bride,—
Though fairer maidens might be found
Among the Alpine hamlets, round:—

But hers were winning charms, that shone
Not in the face and form alone,—
The graceful deed, the gentle speech,
That to the coldest heart can reach.
And Zaphor loved his foreign bride,
As hearts can only love at first,
Before the tares of strife and pride
Among their Eden flowers are nursed:
And, by his tribe, the harvest queen
More loved and honoured ne'er had been
Than she—the wanderer of the west!
Yet ever, on her gentle breast
A silent sorrow seemed to hang;
Perchance around her slumbers sang
The voices of her native streams,—
That murmur through the exile's dreams,
When the heart wanders homeward, reft
Of all, but memory—latest left!
Perchance, from Zaphor's love, she turned
To that by Wolga's waters urned!

    " Whate'er it were, the secret care
That dimmed the brightness of her smile,—
Like winter sunbeams, faint and fair,
It shone on Zaphor's home, the while:
Nor time nor tears can e'er destroy
Her country's gift of hope and joy;
That to its saddest children clings,

Like pleasant sounds to broken strings,—
The ivy of their ruined hearts,
When all life's brighter bloom departs,—
Surviving change and blight and blast,—
Their first possession—and their last!
That gift was hers,—but bright and brief;
She left us, like an early leaf,
That wakes amid the wintry scene,
And falls before the woods are green.
While yet its second summer's glow
Shone on her wedded life, there sped
An arrow from the burning bow,
And laid her beauty with the dead!
And Zaphor might not mourn the fate[20]
That made his dwelling desolate,
And bade his first-born seek in vain
The love she ne'er might find again:—
No! bending o'er her burial sod,
He praised—or tried to praise—his God!
For ever glorious is their lot
On whom disease and time lay not
Their withering touch:—no mortal hand
May summon to the spirit land
The chosen hearts, to whom 'tis given
To fall but by the shafts of heaven!

"So deemed the tribe; and raised her tomb,
With feast and song,—as best became

The heir of such a glorious doom.
But oft, at that young stranger's name,
In after days, their tears would start,—
For she was missed by many a heart.
And Zaphor's days of peace were o'er;
He girt his armour on once more,—
The sword and buckler laid aside
When first he won his foreign bride.
And now he called his warrior band,—
And many a chief and many a land
Had cause to rue the fatal dart
That smote the treasure of his heart.
But less he sought the battle's broil
From hope of victory or spoil,
Than, in its tempest, to forget
His morning star—too early set!

" But even the wounds of love must close,
Before the healing hand of time:—
And, where the light of beauty glows
Upon the Georgian's kindred clime,
He found another bride, whose charms
Recalled him from the din of arms.
Of princely lineage was the dame,
And well a warrior's love might claim:
And Zaphor loved her well, in sooth,—
But not like her who blessed his youth.
Still, as the passing summers shed

New blossoms o'er his early dead,
Around his hearth and home there sprung
The household branches, fair and young,—
But none like that lost wanderer's child
On Zaphor's mountain fortress smiled!

"Oh! wondrous was the beauty given
To that young orphan's form and face;
Perchance our Prophet saw, in heaven,
Some Houri's form of equal grace,—
But never was it found on earth,
Among the maids of mortal birth,
Nor e'er were Houri's glances fraught
With such strange power of early thought,
As kindled in her matchless eye;
And there was more of majesty
Around her steps than e'er was seen
In woman's or in warrior's mien:—
She might have been a crownless queen,
Like captive Tadmor's—lone—alone,
Surviving glory, love and throne,
Yet bearing round her, to the last,
The shadow of an empire past!
For still some darkening shadow blended
With all the glory of her years,—
Perchance her mother's grief descended
To her, the child of love and tears;
Yet stately was the maid, and tall,—

The cedar of her father's hall.
And long her early womanhood
Remained unwon, though not unwooed:—
For princely suitors sought her hand,
The noblest of our mountain land;
But none could reach her sire's demand.
And Zaphor was a worthy sire;—
Though fierce and stormy in his ire,
And ruling less by love than fear,
Yet were his blooming children dear
To him, as, to the mountain bear,
The dwellers of its rocky lair.

"But, for that bright-eyed girl, his heart
Had deeper springs, and purer too:—
It might be that her mother's part
Was given to her, unchanged and true,
As death had left it long ago;
The fountain could not cease to flow,
And on that stately orphan's head,
Its holiest, brightest dews were shed.
But with the father's love was blent
A father's pride;—his high descent,
His princely sons, his Georgian bride,
And daughters blooming by her side,
Were feathers in the balance, weighed
'Gainst gold, beside that orphan maid.—
Ah! oft, such love hath been the seed

Of many a dark and envious deed,
In princely hall and peasants' cot,
Since Joseph's fatal robe was wrought!

"But this fair girl was loved, at home,—
Even by the noble Georgian dame
Who never could forget that from
A Christian land her mother came;
And deemed her, therefore, half a Frank
In blood—and scarcely fit to rank
With her true Moslem daughters; yet,
At times, the matron would regret
That luckless chance, in saddened tone,
And wish the orphan all her own.
And well she might:—for fairer face
Ne'er met a mother's warm embrace,
Than young Dizila's;—such the name
Her sire bestowed—since in a dream,[31]
Before her birth, he saw a star,
That rose above his fortress far,
But wandered—where he could not tell,—
And from its mass, a brightness fell,
That turned to blood;—and Zaphor deemed
That of *her* destiny he dreamed.
But none among our old and wise
Could read the riddle of that night;—
For oft, unsought, unbidden, rise,
Upon the sleeper's startled sight,

The mystic characters of fate,
Though still interpreted too late!
So deemed the father; and between
His hope and fear, that name had been
Bestowed on her—whose Christian mother
Had early called her by another.
That name was long forgotten, now;
But, in Dizila's sunny brow
And fearless glance, her sire might see
The tameless spirit, bright and free,
Of that young mother's western land,—
Though gentle were her smiles, and bland
Her accents, as her mother's were,—
Like silver streams, or summer's air.

" Yet, at the sight of human wrongs,
Her eye would strangely flash, at times,
With fiercer brightness than belongs
To even the eyes of eastern climes;—
And hers, since childhood's early years,
Were woman's eye without its tears,
And woman's heart without its fears!
For she was lone in spirit, ever;
By mountain steep and rushing river
She roamed, with neither friend nor guide
Save her good steed, and by her side
Her trusty poniard bright,—the maid
With her own hands had edged the blade;

For still she bore a skilful part
Alike in man's and woman's art.[28]

"And she than these had nobler skill:
For she had pored upon the pages
That make the Christians wise; yet still
She loved our mountain bards and sages,
And early drank those sacred waters
That seldom cheer Circassia's daughters,—
The ancient wisdom of the hills,
Now found in few and scattered rills,
Where, once, majestic rivers rolled,
Sprung from the Grecian founts of old,
Ere Stamboul was a Turkish hold!
Her Atalik[29] was one whose eye
Had gazed on many a distant sky:
In many a clime his steps had roved;—
'Twas said he looked upon and loved
Her mother, in her native land,
But vainly sued for heart and hand.
And when, his weary wandering past,
He sought Pitzounda's wooded shore,
But only found her grave at last,
The fervour of his youth was o'er!
He had outlived the burning hour;
Yet had Dizila's beauty power
The early-frozen fount to wake,—
He loved her, for her mother's sake,

And, dwelling with the tribe, became
A brother both in heart and name.
And Zaphor, when he lost his mate,
And sought a fearless warrior's fate,
The orphan to that care consigned;
The mourner poured upon her mind
The stores of story, song and thought,
That from his distant land he brought:—
For he was born where sunset shines
On Christian Europe's western shrines.

" The maiden loved him and his lore,
With young affection, pure and free,—
But loved her native mountains more,—
They were her friends from childhood; she
Had gazed upon them, night and day,
And seen the verdure pass away
From field and forest, as the blast
Of Autumn o'er their beauty past.
Her mother's love had left her, ere
She knew its blessed depth; and ne'er
Could stepdame kind or sister dear,
Or all her father's proud affection,
Efface the dreary recollection
That made her still, in woe or mirth,
A stranger, by the household hearth:—
But still the mountains rose before her,
And hung their gleaming glaciers o'er her,

Unchanged, as when her infant eyes
Beheld them mingling with the skies!

"And as her country's hills, she loved
Her country's freedom; and beheld,
With eyes and feelings not unmoved,
The spirit of Pitzounda quelled
By northern gold:—for never steel
Could tame or tire the sleepless zeal
Of bright Abasia! But in vain
Dizila strove to call again
Her father to his country's aid,—
Though high and nobly spoke the maid:
For Zaphor only smiled, and said
That war was not a woman's care,—
And bade her braid her raven hair,
For she might, one day, chance to grace
Some northern chieftain's dwelling-place!
Then, in his daughter's eye there shone
A light that changed the scoffing tone:—
And, when they parted, woe to all,
Serf, son or stranger, in his path,
On whose defenceless head might fall
The tempest of his reckless wrath!—
So, the tired maid had ceased to speak
The burning thought that dyed her cheek,
And buried in her lonely breast
The secret of its proud unrest.

E

" 'Twas when the yellow corn was heaving
Around her, like a golden sea,
And summer's latest tints were leaving
Pitzounda's woods,—when rock and tree
Had caught the solemn light that lies
In the still depth of autumn skies,—
A Moscov prince, with all his train,
Arrived in Zaphor's fair domain:—
And royal was his welcome there,
From martial chief and matron fair.
Lord of ten thousand serfs, his halls
Were seen from that proud city's walls
That, like the fabric of a dream,
Arose by Neva's icy stream,—
To let the coming ages see
How great a tyrant's work can be!
'Twas said the prince was sent upon
A secret embassy,—to bind
More firmly to his master's throne
The mountain tribe: yet some assigned
A gentler errand;—*which* were true,
The prince, alone, and Zaphor knew.
But many a costly gift amazed
Pitzounda's warriors, as they gazed
Upon the stranger's pomp; and long,
In Zaphor's halls, the festive song
Summoned the ever-joyous throng;
And mountain Pshe and shepherd blessed

The coming of the noble guest.
He seemed indeed a stately chief;
With speech more bland and far less brief
Than warrior's words are wont to be,
Yet was his bearing bold and free:
Though still in manhood's early prime,—
And fair, for son of that dim clime
Whose torpid rivers miss the sun,
And fall asleep, the while they run,—
Yet he had shown, in many a field,
The sheen of an unsullied shield.

  " Among his warlike train, there came
A Polish youth, whose race and name
Were all unknown to wealth or fame;
Though not a braver heart was found,
Nor form with nobler beauty crowned,
In all the lands that feed afar
The countless legions of the Czar.
But ah! as if dark Azrael's breath
Had touched them with the taint of death,
His cheek grew pale, his eye grew dim,—
And he had none to care for him!
Well for the stranger, that the hearts
In fair Pitzounda were not all
Chilled by the northern spoiler's arts!
Oh! ever does the tyrant's thrall
Fall, like a polar frost, to bind

The free, sweet fountains of the mind!
Yet springs there are, no power restrains,
That gush beneath their icy chains;
And thus, in Zaphor's hall, was one
Who felt for Poland's wandering son,
And to his couch of anguish brought
Such solace as her nature taught,—
Though few—and they but vassals—came
To share the wild and mystic game[24]
That frights death's messengers away,
Like vultures from the rescued prey.
The young Dizila soothed his pain,
And watched his slumber, till again
His cheek was mantling with a bloom
That had no presage of the tomb.

" And for the maiden's saving care,
He paid her with as true a heart
As ever bowed to beauty's snare,
Or felt the sightless archer's dart:
And that was all that fate had left
The stranger; for the stroke that cleft
His country's ancient sword and crown,
With ruthless force, had shaken down
The antique house from which he sprung,—
Though glory round its ruins hung.
And he, its last, lone blossom, young
In heart and hope, had left afar

His Polish home, to win, in war,
The smiles of fortune, or the grave
That oft awaits the early brave:—
Too young to feel his sword was drawn
For Poland's spoilers,—till the dawn
Of truth upon his spirit broke,
As she, the mountain maiden, spoke
Of all his distant country's tears,
Beneath the conqueror's iron hand!
For he had learned, in happier years,
The language of her mother's land,—
A stream by all the nations tasted,
For ever flowing on, unwasted,
By desert tent and forest home,
By minaret and Christian dome,—
Voice of the palace, field and mart,
And meeting-place of many a heart
Whose homes of birth were far apart.
And such these found it, when the youth
Poured forth, with all the fervent truth
Of the young heart's unchanging mood,
His mingled love and gratitude,—
And young Dizila's accents free
Breathed the deep soul of liberty.

"I know not if the maid returned
The hallowed flame, whose steady gleam'
Within his bosom smiled and burned:—

Such tales shall be the pleasant theme
Of youth and maid, till harp and lute,
In the world's dying days, are mute!—
For fair Dizila's, though less cold
Than other hearts, in higher mould
Was cast,—and seemed too proudly pure,
A thing so perishing and poor
As earthly passion to endure.
Yet tender fancies mixed with high;
And oft the maiden's matchless eye,
Whose starry brightness few could brook,
Would soften to her mother's look,—
As if some shadow came to dim
Its splendour, when she looked on him,
Though why, or whence, that shadow fell
Upon her soul we could not tell.

" ' Queen of the world! whose altars rise
On ice-bound wastes and burning sands,—
Immortal Merem,[35] fair and wise,—
The served and loved of many lands!
Long may our fields and vineyards share
Thy blessing and thy fostering care,
And long our youths and maidens prove
The first in war—the best in love!
For thou wert great, amongst our snows,
Ere yet the Eastern Prophet rose;
And still the summer's golden close

Awakes for thee our festive strains,—
Thine only rite that now remains,
Among the hills where Vinon[36] trod
Victorious for the Christian's God,
Save the grey cross, with garlands drest.—
Return, bright Virgin of the west!'

" So sang Pitzounda's youth, beneath
The twilight's cloudy coronet,—
With mystic dance and votive wreath,
At Merem's sacred feast-time met,
Then, when the autumn moon rose clear,
And the bright balance of the year
Gave day and night an equal reign.
And mingling with the festive train,
The Moscov prince, that eve, was seen;
Though rarely in his land, I ween,
Such worship hailed the harvest queen,—
For she is served, in Christian lands,
With solemn rites and saintly hands.
But well our maidens could divine
The zeal that led him to her shrine,
The plenty-spreading bread to break,
Was for *another* virgin's sake,—
To whom such earthly charms were given
As win our human hearts from heaven.

" For young Dizila came, that night,
Among the joyous dancers, there,

In queenly robes, and gems whose light
Grew dim amid her brighter hair.
No other form, in all the dance,
Had power to fix the Moscov's glance,—
Though many a maiden tried her art
To lure his eye and snare his heart:
No spell could win him from her side,—
Though still the maiden's patriot pride,
Even in the dance, her hand denied.
Oft, 'mid the banquet's stir and glare,
Her furtive glance would wander, where
The festal torches faintly shone,
And the young Polack sat alone,—
And gazed on her, as, from afar,
Some watcher gazes on a star.

" The banquet ceased: the starry hours
Passed, in their silent course, away;
And shone on Zaphor's stately towers
The glory of the rising day.
But still no step, from hall or bower,
Came forth to greet that lovely hour,—
For few of all the garlands, worn
On festal nights, may meet the morn.
Yet she who, in the banquet, shone
The brightest, from her lattice lone
O'er stream and valley looked abroad,
Upon the rising sun, that strode

Like monarch to his throne.   From eyes
So tearless, slumber rarely flies,
Till life's dark shadows round them rise:—
It might be so with her; for now,
The maid hath leaned her marble brow
Upon the snowy hand, to gain
Whose clasp a prince had sued in vain,
And far, in thought, retired apart
To the still chambers of her heart;—
It might be so,—for whatsoe'er
Her dreams, they seemed too deep to hear
A well-known step, though loud and near.

"But why that strange and sudden start,—
As if an arrow reached her heart,—
When but her father's hand is prest
Upon the locks he loved the best?
'And dost thou greet me thus, my child?'—
Old Zaphor said, and proudly smiled
On her—like one who could unfold
Some pleasant tidings, yet untold:—
'I know thy soul, with wisdom fraught,
Was early given to lonely thought,—
For brighter stars have blessed thy view
Than e'er our mountain people knew:
But oh! my beautiful and bright,
Thy mother's God hath heard, for thee,
The prayer I offered, day and night;

And now, my spirit joys to see
The varied honours that await
My daughter, in her wedded state.
Thy years shall not be wasted here,
With some rude chieftain-mountaineer,
Nor shalt thou share, 'mid jealous strife,
The labours of a second wife:—
No! thine the joy, and mine the pride,
To see my girl a prince's bride,—
A Christian chief's, who weds but one,
And proves his faith to her alone;
For now, the noblest of his land,
The princely Paschoff, claims thy hand.'

"Silent and fixed the maiden stood;
There was no change in look or hue,—
Save that, as oft in musing mood,
Her cheek more like to marble grew;
And, in her glance so wildly bright,
There shone a strange and troubled light,
Which, like the summer's lightning, broke
On Zaphor's quiet, as she spoke:—
'What! wed the Moscov?—Father, no!
Thou wouldst not mock thy daughter so!
Though far his name and power outshone
The splendours of the northern throne,
Yet, by the woes our land hath known
Since on its hills the spoiler stood,

And by the still unfrozen blood
Our bravest hearts have poured, in vain,
On mountain gorge or battle-plain,—
I would not bear his northern name,
For Omar's wealth or Ali's fame!
My mother sleeps her quiet sleep,
'Neath yonder cross that crowns the hill;
And if thy lonely visions keep
Of her one blessed memory still—
Like setting sunlight on the wave
That glistens by her lonely grave—
If e'er her love and beauty mild
Thy weariness of life beguiled,
Deal gently with her orphan child!
Play not the Tartar tyrant's part;—
I cannot wed without my heart.'

" It was in vain, the maiden's prayer!
Though love and memory pleaded there,
They could not shake her father's will,—
For Zaphor's pride was stronger still.
' To-morrow's morn, prepare to wed
The Moscov prince: my word is past
Beyond recall'—he sternly said—
' And brightly, girl! thy lot is cast.
Go! bless the peerless charms that won,
For Zaphor's house, so great a son!
Submission best becomes thy sex,

And scruples serve but to perplex
The young:—methinks, thy father's friend
No further praises need commend.
But, girl, if thou wouldst not offend
Against my love, repeat no more
The words of treason;—on our shore
The Moscov rules, with sovereign sway,
And all our wiser chiefs obey
The Czar, who reigns by right divine;
He is my lord—and shall be thine!'

" The maiden heard, and answered not;
And her proud father turned away;—
But Zaphor hath not yet forgot
His daughter's parting look, that day:
So full of high and hopeless thought,
It seemed as if that moment taught
Her soul some dark and fatal truth,
That, from the trusting heart of youth,
Had power love's latest ties to sever,
And leave it desolate for ever!
Oh! little deemed that father, then,
They parted ne'er to meet again!
So, sire and maiden went their way;
And swiftly flew the autumn day,
In cheering labours, that rejoice
The reaper's heart, and wake the voice
Of song. But, when the sun was going,

In regal glory, to his rest,
And his last look of light was glowing
Upon the western mountain's breast,—
Where upward wound a narrow way,
Skirting a torrent's path of spray,
Two warrior youths were seen to speed,
As swift as flies the Tartar steed,
By winter's hungry wolves pursued
Through Ukraine's boundless solitude:
And, as the rocky ridge they gained,
One of the twain a moment reined
His steed, and on the landscape cast
A look that might have been his last,—
So sad, so long, it seemed to be
The dying gaze of memory!
Then onward, through the gathering night,
They swept, like eagles in their flight!

" And there were sleepless eyes, that night,
And looking forth from Zaphor's door,
For her whom morning's coming light
To hearth or board brought never more.
How, when the evening fire was piled,
And joyous faces round him smiled,
The father missed his sweetest child!
But never, from that fatal hour,
Though Zaphor searched, with all his power,
The mountain-paths,—and, far and wide,

The Moscov sought his destined bride,—
Came tidings of our vanished fair;
Save that her dark luxuriant hair
In one bright braided band was found,
Upon her mother's grave-cross bound,[37]
Twined with the mountain-flowers that spread
Above the gentle sleeper's head,—
A matchless offering to the dead!
Perchance it was the sacrifice
Of that young heart's unuttered vow;—
But winter's blast and summer's sighs
Have thinned and blanched the long locks now:
And Zaphor's household mourn no more,—
Their time of search and tears is o'er,
And all seem happy as before.
Yet oft, when festive song and mirth
Are loud around the blazing hearth,
The father's eye in silence seeks
A brow of which his memory speaks,—
Oh! never more to meet his gaze,
As in the light of happier days!
And oft, when autumn's sunset burns
Upon the hills, the chieftain turns
To that lone path she loved so well
To thread, away by wood and dell,—
As if he still might hope to hail
Her snowy steed and floating veil!

" Ah! still her gentle memory twines
About his heart;—she was the child
Of his first love,—whose early shrines
Remain undimmed and undefiled
By all the after taint or crime
That darkened o'er his later time!
And on that father's faded brow
Are furrows—not the work of years:
It may be that his fatal vow
Is washed away with sacred tears,—
But, like the streams that caverns hide,
No eye may mark that silent tide.
For Zaphor is a chieftain, still,
And no less wayward in his will,—
Now, as of old, unused to bend,
And, as of yore, the Moscov's friend.
The harvest feasts no more recall
The princely Paschoff to his hall;
Though many a mountain-suitor there
Hath found a bride, perchance less fair,
But kinder far than her *he* wooed,—
And happier in her lowlier mood.
Our hills the noble Moscov left,
When search and hope alike grew vain;—
Nor only of his bride bereft,—
For, the same eve, his lordly train
Had lost a warrior—never missed
Till morning's beam the mountains kissed.

But, whether gone at morn or eve,
The Polish youth had none to grieve
For him—save some on Cracow's plain,
Who listened for his step in vain,
Or mourned him as in battle slain.
If he with fair Dizila fled—
And how or where their journey sped,—
Or what their after-fate hath been,—
No ear hath heard, no eye hath seen;
But still their mingled memory fills
The songs of minstrels, on our hills!

" The Moscov left us;—but his heart
Went with the wanderer of its choice:
Though soon from memory's depths depart
The echoes of the sweetest voice,—
His love was such as doth not change
With time or absence; for a strange
And nameless cloud had o'er it hung,
And chilled his heart and chained his tongue,
Even while the bride he sought was near.
There was a boding voice of fear
That murmured in his spirit's ear,—
As moans afar the mountain gale
Ere yet it rushes o'er the vale,—
Till maidens asked, in mirthful mood,
If *thus* the Christian warriors wooed!
But some have said,—in other days,

When Servia's sylvan shore he trod,
A maiden of that wandering race
Who own no land and fear no god,
While at her feet the Danube rolled,
In wild and mystic words foretold
That what his spirit most of all
Should worship, *by his hand should fall,*—
And bade him dread the moment, most,
That *brought him near the loved and lost!*
It might have been an idle tale;
Yet Paschoff's cheek would oft grow pale,
While gazing on his chosen one,—
And fears save of the heart are none
For such as he!—But all is past!
And I, to Kazi's chiefs, at last,
In lonely minstrel-guise, relate
The story of our wandering star,—
To trace whose dark mysterious fate
My weary steps have roamed so far."

    *   *   *   *

    The minstrel ceased:—but silence, yet,
Upon the gathered legions hung;
And many a fount of old regret,
In withered bosoms freshly sprung,
Expressed how sorrowing songs recall
The ghosts of buried griefs to all.
And Gusbeg's hand was on his brow,—

F

As if the close of that wild strain
Had woke some chord of woe: but now
The chieftain raised his eyes again;
And said, with aspect mild though pale,
" Minstrel, we thank thee for thy tale!
Time only can reveal the fate
Of her, the lady of thy lay;—
But may a warrior's blessing wait
Upon the gentle wanderer's way,
Who scorned to wed her country's foe,
In all his power and glory's glow!
For thee—a daughter's love reward
At once the atalik and bard!"

The chiefs assented; and there rose
From out the crowd a murmured sound
Like that which stirs the deep repose
Of some old wood, with foliage crowned,
When birds are hushed, and summer eves
Are breathing on its countless leaves.

But Hassan's soul was yet uncharmed;
For they who sing the mystic lay
That soothes the Indian-serpent, armed
With all its fearful power to slay,
Might prove how vain their boasted art,
If tried upon that Lesghian's heart.
Though none among the mountain peers

Had lent the song more earnest ears,
Yet while its sadness woke the tears
Of others, strange suspicious thought
In Hassan's gloomy visage wrought;
And many a stealthy glance he cast
On Kazi's battle-star,—who seemed
A reckless listener, to the last.
But once, the watchful warrior deemed
That, when the father's grief was sung,
Some pang of silent anguish wrung
The stranger's heart, whose sudden thrill
Blanched the young brow with icy chill,
But left it calm and stately still.
Not so his friend:—the Polack's face
Was strangely troubled; and his look
Turned on the bard, with fierce rebuke,—
As if no memory should retrace
The vanished scenes, or minstrel tell
The tale, he knew, perchance, too well.

Dark Hassan saw; yet ne'er revealed
His secret doubts, whate'er they were;
But, from that day, in camp or field,
His eye was ever on the pair;
And o'er his callous nature came
A wondrous change, for one whose heart
Had never known the generous flame
Of love or friendship,—but apart

Lived, like the tiger, in his own
Dark, jealous selfishness alone.
And ever after, where the tide
Of battle bore those matchless friends,
The chief was with them, side by side,
Like one whose veteran sword defends
His children; but, that danger o'er,
The Lesghian's care was seen no more.

*   *   *   *

The Moscov knew his mission done;—
He, too, had listened to the strain
Of that lone mountain-bard, like one
To whom its notes recalled again
Some voice of other times, or scene
Through which his early path had been.
It might be that his memory kept—
As hides the wave the buried bark,—
Some meteor dream, that once had swept
Across his soul,—but left it dark
And cold again, till that wild song—
Like desert winds that sigh among
Forsaken strings—awoke in him
The echoes of his perished years,
And with their chiming, sweet and dim,
Blent tones that told of tombs and tears:
Such shadows o'er his visage past
As only troubled memories cast!

But now he turned him to the bard,
And proffered freely—as became
A northern chief—such bright reward
As they that sing for kings may claim;
And gave, in fair and courtly phrase,
The minstrel's higher meed of praise.

With eye that flashed indignant pride,
But accents calm, the bard replied:—
"The Moscov need not now be told
How well my wearied country knows
The power that dwells in strangers' gold,—
But I have felt, and shared, her woes.
Take—take thy glittering gift away,—
Such ne'er inspired a native lay;—
For courteous speech of thine, I owe
A minstrel's thanks; but, chieftain, know
That this unfettered lyre of mine
Was never tuned for thee or thine!"
The Moscov answered by a smile,
That spoke his secret scorn, or guile;
Then to the chiefs of Kazi bent
In parting form;—but, ere he went,
Again the minstrel spoke:—"Adieu,
Most noble Paschoff!—may the doom
So darkly spoken prove untrue!—
For, ne'er, beneath the waving plume
Of Christian knight, or turban's fold,
Beat heart than thine more true and bold!"

" And who art thou?" dark Hassan cried,
" Who canst assume the patriot air
So well,—though late, it seems, allied
With that Abasian traitor:—where,
In all the fields of freedom's war,
Hath flashed that idle scimitar,
Which seems to mock thy tuneful lyre?
Oh! if, amid the strife of swords,
Thy blade had gleamed with half the fire
That beams upon thy minstrel-chords,—
It might have served our country, more
Than all the rocks that guard her shore!
But, say! what land hath sent thee forth?
Thou art not ours;—thy speech and mien
Betray the hidden Nazarene,
Born in the far and frozen north,
Or 'neath the dew of western skies,—
Then, wherefore thus in Moslem guise?"

" Lesghian! thy words are true,—my land
Is far away; but never nation,
From Athens' early desolation,
To Poland's last heroic band,
Had braver hearts or brighter fame
Than that far western isle can claim.
And well, methinks, her wandering son
May wear the garb of any race
That even through thunder-clouds hath won

A glimpse of freedom's angel face!
Oh! that *her* glorious eye might shine
Upon the land that once was mine!—
But, chief! methinks we two have met,
In other years:—rememberest, yet,
The silent and forsaken plains,
Where the great pyramids have flung
Their mighty shadows, since the fanes
Of Carnak and the Nile were young,—
Yet, never looked on pomp or fame
Like his, the Prince of Fire,[20] whose path
Was like the lightning's, marked in flame,
And making deserts in its wrath?
There, on *that* desert's lonely marge,—
Where the old crescent's pride went down,
Before the thunder of his charge,—
There, when the battle's fiery frown
Was, in the golden sunset, past,
Chief of the hills,—we parted last!"
So spake the bard, and, speaking, flung
The mantle back that o'er him hung,
And stood, with cuirass, spear and shield,
Armed like a warrior for the field!
" And are there none," he cried, " who know
" Cuzali? Do the hosts forget
The chief who led them, long ago,
When first in battle shock they met

The Moscov?—we were victors then,—
I come to share such fields again!"

A thousand tongues take up the name,—
A thousand hearts the hero own,
Who 'mid their hills had conquered fame :—
His early tale was all unknown,—
Save that Pitzounda's traitor tribe
Were his first brothers in the land,—
But when, to gain the northern bribe,
They flung aside the patriot band,
He left their ranks, and led the free
Who battled, still, for liberty.
So, long Ouzali's fame had been
Among the tribes; since first he bore
That sacred gift of Stamboul's queen,
The love-wrought banner, to their shore,
And taught their chiefs the sacred vow
That bound their banded thousands now.

At length, the crowd's wild greeting past,
Came Hassan, of the princes last,
And gazed upon the stranger's face
As one who seeks an ancient trace—
The heart's old pathway; till he grasped,
And, like a long-lost treasure, clasped
The only hand to which he owed
A debt unpaid, save that of God!

For friends are few, in time of need,—
And *he* had found them few indeed:
But once, in battle's wildest strife,
Cuzali saved the Lesghian's life;
And—as the hidden spring that flows
Through desert spots, that else had been
Barren and desolate, bestows
A glorious gift of living green,—
So had the memory of that deed
To his dark soul, in silence, given
A blessed token, that might plead
Not all in vain the cause of heaven,—
And to the world, at last, restore
The bread that seemed on waters flung:
For in that silent clasp was more
Than ever fell from mortal tongue;
And oft to glorious bloom hath grown
The seed in thorny deserts sown!

And now Cuzali spoke once more,
And told them how, o'er land and main,
His steps had been on every shore,
To plead their cause—but plead in vain:
For years had brought the crescent low,—
And Europe's ear was deaf and cold
To every voice that spoke of woe,
And spoke not, too, of power or gold,
Since Poland's banner ceased to be

The last bright star of chivalry.
" And is it so?" brave Gusbeg cried,—
" Then let the battle be our own!
Let cold or coward hearts confide
In aid from foreign sword or throne,—
I would not owe my country's weal
To other than her own bright steel:
Our swords are good—our cause is just—
Be God and these our only trust!"

Scarce ceased his accents on the ear,
When, rushing down the mountain-steep,
With waving flag and shining spear,
And swift as wintry torrents sweep,
A warrior came: his burnished mail
Was dim with dust,—and large and pale
The foam-flakes on his gallant steed,
That told of far and fearful speed.
And well the eye of Gusbeg knew
Azim the swift, his youngest son,—
The flower of all his house, save one
Who slumbered where the cypress grew,
But in his heart kept open still
A void no other name could fill.

The boy who came was fair and young;
And, as his charger nearer drew,
The reins upon the neck he threw,

And lightly from the saddle sprung.
Before his steps, the eager crowd
Parted, as parts the waveless main,
By some deep-laden galley ploughed
With furrows, soon to close again:—
For all, in silence, pressed to hear
His message to the public ear.
And briefly were his greetings made,
As to the gathered chiefs he said:
"Princes, arise! by Kouban's stream,
The Cossack strings his deadly bow,
And far the lifted lances gleam,—
There is no time for council, now.
Despite the Russian's proffered peace,—
Faithless alike to foe and friend—
His conquering legions still increase,
And now, in stealthy silence, bend
Their march upon the lovely valley
And ruined strength of Soudjouk Kalé.
Thus far their counsels to discern,
My soul hath brooked the traitor's wile,—
But they who war with wolves must learn
To match them in their ruthless guile:—
When in Crimea's desert, last,
The glowworm lit her vesper lamp,
An unsuspected spy, I passed
In safety through the Moscov camp;
And thence, with eager haste, have sped,

The tidings in our land to spread,
And bid my country's hosts prepare
Against some dark and fatal snare."

As when, by some lone fisher's hearth,
His lowly friends have met, to cheer
The winter's eve with song and mirth,
Though storms are loud and skies are drear,—
If, from the ocean, rolling nigh,
Comes, mingled with the northern blast,
The drowning seaman's stifled cry,
Whose hapless bark the billows cast
On rocks or sands—the treacherous grave
Of many a wanderer of the wave,—
All rush abroad, to see and save,
Till hearth and home are silent left,
As if of all their living reft;—
So was that vale deserted, now,
Ere yet the sun, whose early light
Shone on the coming herald's brow,
Had reached the eastern mountain's height:
The ancient trees stood, still and green,
In their broad shadow, as they grew,
Ere yet that bannered host were seen,—
Nor tent nor martial form in view;
For swift as whirlwinds on the plain,—
Or rivers swelled by mountain rain,

When summer breathes upon the snow,—
The sons of Kazi come and go!

  *   *   *   *

'Twas midnight: upon Soudjouk's bay
The summer moon shone full and bright,
And broad the slumbering Euxine lay
Beneath the calm and cloudless light,—
Which to its waveless breast had given
The glory both of earth and heaven.
For all things seen were mirrored there,—
From starry sky and moonlight fair,
To the dark mountains, high and steep,
That stood like watchers o'er the deep,—
Robed, now, in forests green and old,—
Now, crowned with glaciers white and cold,
Or rocky summits bare and bold,
Like relics of an early world
Of old to hopeless ruin hurled,—
That, in their barren strength, frowned on
When all its fairer things were gone.
There, peak on peak sublimely soared,
In rival grandeur,—till in vain
Had even the eagle's eye explored
The limit of their boundless chain,—
With many a deep and wild ravine
And lovely valley spread between.

But downward sloping to the bay,
The fairest of those valleys lay,—
Where summer's night seemed turned to day.
For not the full-orbed moon alone
Upon its scattered hamlets shone,—
But frequent gleams of fiercer light,
From signal fires on every height;
And martial echoes, from afar,
Proclaimed the swift approach of war.
And sights and sounds like these were most
Where a dismantled fortress rose,—
The only barrier of the coast
As yet unwon by Kazi's foes:
For, though the eagle's wing had swept
Twice o'er its towers, yet fate had kept
Them sacred, in their ruined strength,
To be more dearly won, at length.
Oh, fatal towers! the hands that raised
Their glory, perished, while they gazed:
Within those sheltering walls arose
A deadlier foe than northern foes,—
Pale Pestilence, with livid brand,
Who held the keep, and scourged the land,—
Till native sinews, trembling, sought
To raze what native sinews wrought;
And bastion rent and shattered frame
Still told of *how* that ruin came:—
Alas! the deadly dust alone

That Milton says was made in heaven,
By rebel-angels—long o'erthrown,
And into utter darkness driven,
Could, in one wasteful moment, mar
The strength that baffled time and war!

But, now, around those ruined walls,
The measured tread of sentry falls,
Distinct in midnight's lonely hour;
And, resting by the shattered tower,
With watchwords muttered deep and low,
And slumbers such as warriors know
Who wait for morning or the foe,
Are met the bravest of the land,—
The Hadji Gusbeg's gallant band;
For ever theirs the doubtful post
Where hope is least, and danger most.
And many a tribe and many a chief
Reposed, that night, by Soudjouk's bay;
The anxious hours were few and brief
Between them and the battle-day:—
The sunset, as it gilded o'er
The summits of that wooded shore,
Had flashed upon the swift advance
Of Moscov steel and Cossack lance,—
And now, upon the rocky zone
That seemed around the valley thrown,
The nearest of their watchfires shone.

There was a far and silent spot—
Between a forest and the sea—
Where sound of living voice was not,
Save when a murmur, fitfully,
Like night wind sighing through the pines,
Rose from the Moscov's sleepless lines.
And there, in silent vigil, stood,
Amid the moonlit solitude,
The undivided brothers,—so
The pair, whose kindred none might know,
Were named, alike by friend and foe.
The one had fixed his radiant eyes
Upon what seemed their native skies,—
For his was still the tone and air
Of those whose only home is there;
But the young Polack's eye was dim,
With sadly gazing upon him.

He spoke, at length:—"To-morrow's morn
May bring us death;—hast thou no fear?
Nay, look not on me thus in scorn,—
I would not that another ear
Than thine should hear my tongue avow
The terrors that oppress me now!
But thou hast seen my spirit tried,
In scenes of peril, by thy side,
Yet never saw it quail or shrink,
Or turn to fly, or pause to think,

Even on destruction's yawning brink,—
Though every danger shared by thee
Brought more than double dread to me.
Oh! now, there hangs a warning weight
Upon me—like the hand of fate—
Even as the monarch shook, of old,
Before the mystic scroll that told
His doom;—and oft a funeral knell
Upon my spirit's ear hath pealed,—
Whate'er it bodes the morn may tell—
Would it were past, and all revealed!
For fate hath not a doom so drear
As this uncertainty of fear!"

His friend replied, in accents low,
That spoke of wisdom blent with woe:—
"I know not wherefore—but, at times,
When musing on the woes and crimes
That have around my being prest,
There wakes, within this weary breast,
A longing for the dreamless rest
Of Zaca's[40] creed—to which is given
Nor fear of hell nor hope of heaven,—
As if such dreamless sleep alone
Could heal the sorrow life hath known!
And, brave and true as I have found thee,
Well may *thy* soul be weary, too,—
'Tis from the horrors that surround thee

G

That these thy bodings came and grew:
For thou hast shared the fatal years
That filled our land with blood and tears,—
And darker still the prospect grows,
And laden with yet heavier woes!
Or, doth thy pining spirit yearn
To see its early home?—Return!
Thy father's hearth awaits thee yet,—
Thy mother's heart can ne'er forget,—
Oh! fly the terrors of our shore,
And find that peaceful home, once more;
And let thy happier years efface
From memory every lingering trace
Of all that bound thee to our race!"

" Then, wilt *thou* share my Polish home,
And bless my kindred with the light
Of thy bright presence?   Dearest, come,—
And leave the fields of fear and fight!
My country's hope hath long been lost,
And freedom flies her fated coast;
But green her woods are waving, still,
As in Jagellon's days—and hill
And valley shall seem free and fair
To me, beloved! when thou art there."
Strange were the watcher's words, in sooth,
Addressed to such a martial youth;
But midnight is the time for truth,—

And, in the glance of love that now
Was resting on the speaker's brow,
There shone a soul more pure and true
Than man's rude nature ever knew;
Though high resolve and fixed despair,
Beyond both words and tears, were there.

Silent, awhile, Dizila stood;
Then pointed upwards, to the star
That now, above the eastern wood
Shone, like a beacon, bright and far,—
And said:—" Or ere yon planet's light
Returns, to lead the hosts of night
On their bright journey, I shall be
In the far land where all are free!
Earth hath no more a home for me;—
I left, beside my father's hearth,
The smile of childhood's cloudless mirth,—
I shed, upon my mother's grave,
The latest tears that ere should lave
These weary eyes: all else that heaven
To life had promised, or had given,
I on my country's altar laid,
A votive offering freely made:
The offering may be vain—but none
Shall tear it from the altar stone!
Ask then no more what is not mine:
But oh! revoke the generous vow

That made my wayward fortunes thine,—
I bless thee, and restore it, now!
Blest and unbroken, may it prove
To thee the pledge of happier love,—
Some household lamp, whose gentle light
Shall all thy changeless faith requite!
But when, in some far future time,
The prize of freedom crowns thy clime,
(For, yet, that glorious day shall be,—
And, brother! mayst *thou* live to see!)
Think of thine early dreams and me!
Go—and be happy!" " Never, never!"
The Pole replied,—" we may not sever!
For once thy words are vainly spoken,—
The vow is in my heart, unbroken:
In good or ill, whate'er betide,
My chosen path is by *thy* side!"

As when, through autumn's misty veil,
The sun breaks forth in morning splendour,
Till highest peak and deepest dale
Receive his smile so brightly tender,
Till suddenly the cloudy screen,
From the cold mountains, falls between,—
So briefly bright the joy whose glow
Lit up Dizila's brow of snow,—
The last her heart might ever know!
And when it passed, her visage wore

A deeper sadness than before.
" Ah! friend and brother of the past!
How hath thy heart its riches cast
On one who wronged a love so true,
Because its worth she never knew
Till now;—like him who found the pile
Of treasure, in the Serpent's Isle,⁴¹
And bore a few dim pearls away,
Nor dreamed that diamonds deeper lay!"

She ceased:—for, as on Soudjouk rose
The purple of the summer dawn,
The mountain warriors and their foes
Awoke to strife, from brief repose;
And scarce the shades of night were drawn,
Ere pealed the Moscov's signal-gun,
That told the hours of vigil done.
Then loud the bugle's call was rung,
And banners to the breeze were flung;
And chiefs their rival skill displayed,
To form the battle's dread array,—
But Cossack lance and mountain blade,
As wont, began the fight that day.

Hark, to the cannon's ceaseless thunder!
Hark, to the Kazi's charging cheer,
That wakes at once the fear and wonder
Of all the hostile hearts that hear!

And, mingling with that mighty peal,
Comes the loud clang of mountain steel:
For, as the avalanche, let loose
From the dark brow of Elberous,
Sweeps down o'er forest, stream and rock,
With lightning-speed and thunder-shock,—
So come, at once, the battle cry
And headlong charge of Attéghéi!⁴³

But on the Moscov legions press,
In numbers countless as the sands
That, in the eastern wilderness,
O'erwhelm the luckless pilgrim-bands.
Onward they press; for many a coast
Hath sent its sons to swell that host,
And show the mountain-tribes how far
Can reach the sceptre of the Czar.
There, are Siberia's hardy sons,—
The children of the conquering Huns,—
The peasant from the Caspian's side,—
The serf from near the Baltic's tide,—
And fair Tchernemorsky's rival spear,
The hatred of the mountaineer,—
All the deep tide of northern power
Turned full on Soudjouk's ruined tower!
In Europe's matchless arms arrayed,
Their legions came; but few, I ween,
Without the cannon's murderous aid,

The laurels of that day had been:—
For never was the proudest hold
Of Moslem power or Christian gold
Defended with more desperate power,
Than Soudjouk-Kalé's ruined tower.
But little can the force avail
Of mountain warriors, that oppose,
Against such thunder-bearing foes,
Their dauntless breasts and shining mail!
Alas, for Sparta's boasted walls!—
How fast the living rampart falls,
Before the dark destroyer, known
To Europe's later fields alone!

But, oh! not unavenged they fall,—
For many a noble sire and dame
Shall weep the son who left their hall,
To win a northern warrior's fame;—
And many a Polish maiden, far
By Warsaw's Vistula, shall mourn
The peasant from his country torn,
To perish in a tyrant's war.
For every rent and blackened stone
Around that ruined fortress strown,
A fearful price of blood was paid;—
And each Circassian warrior's blade
Like Death's own sickle seemed to play
In the dread reaping of that day.

Inch after inch the field was won;
And though the morning's rising sun
Looked on the fiery fight begun,
Yet when, at eve, his setting beams
Were cast on Soudjouk's hills and streams,
The bloody work was still undone.

But when the tottering tower gave way,
Before the cannon's fiery play,—
That to a like destruction swept
The warriors and the walls they kept,—
By whelming force of numbers driven
From ruined ramparts, thunder-riven,
Their bravest fallen,—the last resource
Remaining for their broken force
Was the far mountain-wild;—and, slow,
Before the scarce pursuing foe,
With few to fly and none to yield,
The weary warriors left the field.

But who are these, that, on the plain,
Last of that broken host remain,—
While, round their feeble phalanx close
The countless hosts of Moscov foes?
Still, through the mass of hate and wrath,
Their falchions ope a bloody path,—
For all unmatched with spear or brand,
Were Hadji Gusbeg's gallant band!

Their chief had fallen:—but round him pressed
The bravest of his spears and best,—
With remnants from the legions left,
And chiefs, of friends and followers reft,—
All boldly bent to bear away
The form that now seemed only clay;—
But scorn be on the craven's head
Who leaves behind the noble dead![45]
And never chief was, by his ranks,
More prized, since him whom western Franks
Have mourned so long and loved so well,
Than gallant Gusbeg, when he fell.

High o'er him, one, with snowy hand,
Upheld the banner of his land,—
Oh! never braved the battle's storm
A lovelier face or fairer form!
Long years, and well, his sword had proved
How truly and how much he loved
His country's freedom;—but, *that* day,
Not even the Pshe, in hottest fray,
Nor Hassan's sword, nor Nirsis' spear—
And chief and Tartar both were near,—
Had half such reckless valour shown,
Or half such desperate peril known,
As he, the Kazi's battle star,
When bearing, through the waves of war,
From Soudjouk's rent and tottering tower,

That flag of union and of power!
But not alone, the deed was done;
Perils and toils were shared by one
Whom blood nor danger could divide,
A moment, from that brother's side.
Ah! stranger of the snowy brow,
A deadlier peril waits thee, now!
A thousand swords are turned on thee,—
Fling—fling the banner down, and flee!
Behold a chieftain forward rush,
Amid the momentary hush
That comes upon the battle's din,—
As falls, at times, the tempest's breath
To sudden silence, deep as death,
Ere louder, wilder blasts begin!—
'Tis princely Paschoff bids them yield,
Nor deeper dye a sanguine field.

Bold flashing eyes and gleaming swords
Alone made answer to his words.
The Moscov saw them not; for, then,
Amid that group of martial men,
One face had caught his eager eye,—
Was it some dream of memory,
With happier scenes and feelings fraught,
Its sad but glorious beauty brought?
Or some low whisper of the heart,
That, 'mid the tumult, made him start?

Yet, loud again his summons came,—
" Yield! warriors, yield!—in mercy's name!"
" What! yield to thee?" the Polack cried,—
For well he marked the Moscov's eyes,
And read them with a rebel's pride
And rival's hate,—" no, prince of spies,
Rather than yield to northern slaves,
We go to share our brethren's graves!"

Like one who felt some hidden chord
Of anger touched, proud Paschoff's sword
Flashed in the air, with sudden flame;
But, quick as thought, a fairer frame
Between its destined victim came
And that descending blade;—the stroke
Fulfilled the dark prophetic charge
Which, by the Danube's storied marge,
The wandering child of Sinti" spoke:
For, in the banner-bearer's breast
The fatal weapon found its rest!

The Moscov stood in dread amaze,—
Till, as he caught the upward gaze
Of that still glorious eye, there rose
A cry that startled friends and foes;
No mortal utterance may retrace
The pang which in that moment smote
On Paschoff's heart,—nor years efface

The fiery characters it wrote
On memory's tablets!   Could it be?
And was that stranger warrior *she*—
The flower his heart had held so dear,—
The lost one, whom to meet again,
And woo then, haply, not in vain—
Had been, through many a lonely year
And varied scene of peace and war,
Life's beacon-light and polar star?
Oh! lot by ruthless fortune cast!
Had she, the sought through many a land,
Been given to his search, at last,
To perish by his own doomed hand?
Was he like *him* who toiled, in vain,
The stone of mystic power to gain,
And found it, blent with common clay,
So, flung the priceless prize away,—
And only knew its value, when
No power could win it back again?—
Woe for the early-doomed of fate,
And for the hearts that wake too late!

Scarce had that cry from Paschoff broke,
Ere Hassan's swift avenging stroke
Had stretched him on the gory plain,
Mixed, but not numbered, with the slain:
Then, o'er his prostrate form, the strife
Awoke again to fiercer life,

And wilder raged the wild affray
Whose carnage closed that bloody day.

But motionless the Polack stood,
Amid that warring multitude,—
Like her whose voiceless woes, of yore,
Were sung on Hellas' classic shore,
By sudden sorrow turned to stone:—
Ah! well had this one blow repaid
The slaughters of his Polish blade!
For all the powers that life could own,
Of strength, or hope, or fear, were fled,—
And vengeance' very self was dead!
He saw but, in that fatal field,
The form that *was* his living shield;
Felt nothing but her dying grasp—
Undying love was in its clasp—
As, in his faint and heedless hold,
She placed the banner's starry fold,
That now the swiftly-rushing tide
From her own bosom darkly dyed;—
For, in that young heart's latest thrill,
Her friend and country mingled, still!

All power of parting speech was past,—
But on his brow the maiden cast
A long bright look—it was her last,—
Save one—that wandered far away,

Where now the latest beams of day
Were fading from the western height,—
As if some old but pleasant dream
Shed o'er her soul a dying gleam!
But ere the herald star of night
Shone through the gathered clouds—still cleft
By the bright track the sun had left—
For ever closed that glorious eye,
And sank the " Star of Attéghéi!"

And round the moveless Pole arose
The sounds of a lost battle's close,—
Afar the deadly musket flashed,
And loudly shield and sabre clashed:
But still one lifted hand displayed
The blood-stained banner,—in whose shade
That early sleeper, to his breast,
Was, by the other, strongly prest.
Oh! was it his to live, and mourn
Above that slumberer's timeless urn,—
To feel that when life's latest years
Had sealed or dried the fount of tears,
Time had no power, the world no dross,
To pay the young heart's early loss?
No!—Allah sent a better fate
For faith so pure and love so great!—
Though thick as winter's hail around him,—
The Moscov shot and Cossack dart

Passed harmless by that faithful heart;
Yet, when his warrior brethren found him,
The viewless spirit's icy hand
Had done the work of shaft and brand!
The rider of the battle-storm
Had left the fair unwounded form
A trophy of yet mightier power
Than *his*, in that victorious hour!
Lo! human love had triumphed there,—
And, when his power of life was past,
Had kept the still unparted pair
All lovely to the last;
For mortal pain had left no trace
On either fair unfurrowed face!

How passed the Polack to his rest—
Or whence the viewless arrow flew
That lulled him on his lady's breast—
The mountain warriors never knew.
But there they found him, pale and cold,
Bearing their starry banner still;—
And scarcely life could loose the hold
That death had made so stern and chill:
But with the clasp that clung around
Dizila's form, their strength was vain,—
Oh! that which dying love hath bound
No mortal hand may loose again!

And sure the love was strong and strange
Where death itself could bring no change!

*   *   *   *

The battle's latest sound is past;—
And hushed the valley lies, beneath
The shade of midnight's mantle, cast
Upon a field of fear and death:
Whence, though by numbers backward borne,
The mountain remnant, weak and worn,
With brave Cuzali's timely aid,
(Too late, alas! to see, or save
His loved one's bridal of the grave!)
Regained their distant forest's shade:—
All but the Tartar;—lingering on
Where foes were fierce and friends were gone,
Like one who felt his fate was near—
Beyond the touch of hope or fear—
He fell as Tartar chief should fall,
Though fighting for a stranger's land:
With haughty heart and bloody hand,
Alike despising Christian thrall
And Christian mercy, in the pride
Of his dark fathers, Nirsis died!
And all the trophy that remains,
To pay the northern conqueror's pains,
Is that misshapen ruined heap
That once was Soudjouk's castle-keep!

Oh! many a lovely harvest moon,
And many a glorious summer's noon,
Have shone upon that rocky coast
Since Soudjouk's fort and field were lost:—
But still on ruin, rock and bay,
The midnight moonbeams sleep, or play,
As bright as, in their early glow,
On Sidon's temples, long ago![45]

And still the northern standard flies
Above those rent and ruined towers;
But still the mountain race defies
The Czar, and all his warlike powers,—
As mountain pines defy the blast:
Though time and sword and fire have past
O'er that once-fair, but fated, vale,
And scattered to the stream and gale
The ashes of its brightest homes,—
Yet, where the thundering torrent foams
Beside the Alpine eagle's nest,
Its sons have found a surer rest.
And winter star and summer sun
Have seen as glorious battles won,
For freedom, as the Switzer spears
Achieved, in Uri's proudest years!

And still the mountain people cherish,
In all their years of wasting war,

H

As of a ray too bright to perish,
The memory of their fallen star,—
And his who loved its light so well;—
For Kasi's youths and maids can tell
The tale by life so long concealed,
But which the grave, at length, revealed.
And still, when minstrels wake the lyre,
By sacred tree or festal fire,
Their wondrous love and stainless fame
Its saddest, sweetest breathings claim;
Till o'er Cuzali's eagle gaze
There comes a dim and darkening haze,
And maidens weep and warriors sigh,
And stands the tear in Gusbeg's eye,—
For Gusbeg lives, if not so gay
As when he led the mountain spears,
As true and bold as in that day
Whose scars his gallant bosom bears.
And he hath seen his children fall,
Nor wept above each early pall,—
Beheld his home in ruins laid,
And firmer grasped his battle-blade;—
But still the memory of the maid
And youth, whose wondrous story shed
Such glory o'er the band he led,
Beneath the gathered snow of years,
Can stir again his childhood's tears!

But one there is, who weeps not:—tear
Hath never dimmed the fiery eye
Of Hassan! But his Lesghian spear
Hath now a deeper, darker dye.
For never do the Kazi meet
Their foes, in conquest or defeat,
But thoughts of vengeance fire the brave
For her who died—in vain—to save
The youth who shares her early grave!
They nerve the warrior's arm to smite,—
They wing the bullet's deadly flight;
But Hassan's blade and Hassan's blow
Are ever deadliest to the foe,—
And that bright blade hath left but *one*
Of all its vengeful tasks undone,
For ill-starred Paschoff is the first,
And last, who e'er outlived its thirst!

But never, since that hour of doom,
The prince beheld his home again,
And never more his knightly plume
Was met in camp or courtly train;—
His very name is known no more
But in the page that speaks of yore.
Pale silence sits within his halls,
And weeds grow by their lonely walls:—
For he was last of all his race,
And there is none to take his place!

But in a convent old and grey,
Mid Sinai's deserts far away,—
Whose barren wastes, of changeless stone,
And rocks, in shapeless ruin strown,
Seem as to endless silence awed,
Since last they heard the voice of God,—
A pilgrim, from the northern shore,
Received the words of truth and grace
From one whose wasted visage wore,
He thought, the lines of Paschoff's face.
And yet he gazed, and marvelled much
That time's decay or sorrow's touch
Could wither up that lordly brow
To be the thing he looked on, now.
Perchance the broken-hearted sought—
And found—amid the desert's drought,
More healing waters than the wave
Which Lethe's fabled fountain gave;—
Such waters sweeten oft the gloom,
Amid life's wastes—or near its tomb!

There is a grave, all green and lone,
On rocky Soudjouk's utmost bound,—
With flowers of mountain-birth o'ergrown,
And snows above and woods around;
And hostile feet have broken not
The silence of that lonely spot:—
But there, when morning gilds the steep,

The mountain eagles upward sweep;
And there, when evening's latest glow
Is fading from the heights of snow,
Two aged warriors meet, at times,—
The sons of widely-severed climes
Are they; the one, through memory's glass,
Sees palm-trees wave and camels pass,—
The other marks how spring-times smile
On the green hills of Erin's isle.
Nor less contrasted are their minds,—
Yet, in that grave, each warrior finds
The altar of a friendship, rare
And true as theirs who slumber there:
For, since they laid that beauteous pair
To rest, beneath the mountain mould,
Have Hassan and Cuzali been
As brothers;—days and years have rolled
Away, and left their friendship green.
And many a danger they have shared,—
And many a deed of valour dared,—
But oft, from battles won or lost,
From mountain camp or distant coast,
They come, through forest and o'er wave,
To gaze upon that lonely grave!
There, 'mid the hush of nature, sleeps
The flower whom still her country weeps,—
There sleeps the heart that loved her best
In life; the war shall break their rest

No more—*their* peace is purchased, now;—
Oh! well the Pole hath kept his vow!
And well it *is* with loving hearts,
Whom neither death nor distance parts!

Dizila's grave is far away
From father's hearth and mother's urn,—
And Zaphor, at the close of day,
Looks forth no more for her return!
For fame hath told his daughter's tale,
And time hath hushed her kindred's wail.
And mourner's tear or mourner's word
From Zaphor none have seen or heard:—
Yet oft, 'tis said, his midnight dream
Hath broken murmurs, that would seem
To tell of wanderings sweet and far,
Love-lighted by his long-lost star,—
The star that set in that far valley
Beside the ruined Soudjouk-Kalé.

*   *   *   *

My song hath been more sad than sweet!—
But now the strain hath reached its close:
Muse of my country! at thy feet
I leave the lyre;—to thee it owes
At least its sorrow,—if no more
Of thine hath touched its tuneless strings.
But wouldst thou wake, upon our shore,

Some harp like those that spoke, of yore,
Beside the fairy-haunted springs,—
Its voice, like freedom's trumpet-tone,
Might sound in Europe's startled ear,—
To summon freedom's soldiers on,
Ere by high mount and valley lone
The banner of the spoiler wave,
And Aboun be her children's grave!
Yet, if there be no sword to save,
Nor bard to sing, nor heart to hear,—
Strength to thine own bright shield and spear,
Land of the Attéghéi! Thou bearest
A banner of that verdant hue
Which to my country's hills is dearest;
And it may be that in thee, too,
Are found such brave and gifted hearts
As hers:—but better fortune smile
On them than ever blessed the isle!
And thus a humble minstrel parts
From a proud theme;—but as the song
Is feeble, may the prayer be strong!

NOTES

TO THE STAR OF ATTÉGHÉI.

Note 1, page 3.

The ruins of many Grecian cities, and of numerous structures of the Middle Ages, are found in the Caucasian provinces,—and particularly in Circassia.

Note 2, page 3.

Circassia is said to have been peopled by a colony from Troy.

Note 3, page 4.

A stream of Circassia,—much admired for the variety and beauty of the wild flowers which adorn its banks.

Note 4, page 4.

The Circassians call themselves by no other name than that of Attéghéi; which implies a people inhabiting a mountainous country, near the sea-coast,—Atté being a defile, and Ghéi the sea. —*Spencer's Travels in Circassia.*

Note 5, page 5.

Twelve golden stars and three arrows, on a green ground, form the standard of the Circassian tribes united against Russia. It is called, in their language, Sangiac-Sheriff.

Note 6, page 5.

The Circassians were Christians, before their conversion to Mohammedanism; and Christianity is said to have been planted among them by some Crusaders, who found their way into that country. Many ancient stone crosses which still remain, among the mountains, are supposed to mark the graves of these wanderers.

Note 7, page 5.

The Circassians were, formerly, subject to the Khans of the Crimea; but they threw off the yoke, and expelled the Tartars from their country, about the end of the seventeenth century.

Note 8, page 7.

A district of Abasia; where the Russians have erected a fortress, within the ruins of an ancient Greek city.

Note 9, page 8.

A name common to all the Circassian tribes.

Note 10, page 10.

The Turkish name of the Caucasus.

Note 11, page 11.

The Circassian warriors wear a kind of armour, which is said to resemble that worn by the knights of the Middle Ages.

Note 12, page 14.

Some suppose Circassia to have been the ancient Colchis.

Note 13, page 14.

The profession of a minstrel is said to be as common, and as much respected, in the Caucasian provinces, as it was once in Europe.

Note 14, page 14.

See Spencer's Travels in Circassia.

Note 15, page 16.

Like the Tartars, the Circassians conceal their dwellings behind embankments, or clusters of trees.

Note 16, page 16.

One of the principal tribes in the Circassian confederacy.

Note 17, page 18.

It is said that the Sangiac-Shariff was the work of a Circassian princess, occupying a high station in Constantinople.

Note 18, page 20.

Mkinvera, like Elberous, is a name generally applied by the natives to the highest summits of the Caucasus.

Note 19, page 21.

Djamboulet Guérai; whose heroic deeds are the favourite theme of all the wandering musicians in the Caucasus. He was swept away, together with thousands of his countrymen, by the

plague, which the Turks introduced into the country, in 1816.—
Spencer's Travels.

Note 20, page 22.

The translation of a Circassian poem, on this subject, may
be found in the second volume of Spencer's Travels.

Note 21, page 22.

It is well known that one of the Chiefs of the Mamelukes
escaped the general massacre, by the swiftness and agility of his
horse.—[It is now, also, known that several—perhaps many—of
the Mamelukes escaped the massacre of their body, by the con-
trivance of the Pasha, himself, and others; and one of the sur-
vivors, a favourite of the prince, died, not many weeks ago, at
Cairo.—Ed.]

Note 22, page 23.

It is said that this chief—whose devotion to the cause of his
country has been so often and so honourably mentioned by recent
travellers—finding his youngest and favourite son unwilling to
take up arms, compelled him to do so by threats and reproaches;
but the youth fell, in his first battle.

Note 23, page 23.

This colour is peculiar to the Circassian nobility.

Note 24, page 30.

Mithridates.—The previous lines allude to the Macedonian con-
queror. The Persians call the Caucasus the Barrier of Alexander,
because there the conqueror received his first check, from the
valour of the natives.

Note 25, page 30.

Zoroaster is said to have taken refuge in the Caucasus, from
the persecutions raised against him, on account of his peculiar
doctrines.

Note 26, page 32.

Every stranger, travelling in Circassia, is required to have a
native friend, called his Konak, who is answerable for his actions
while in that country.

Note 27, page 33.

One of the Icelandic Skalds, who had killed the son of a
Scandinavian monarch, is said to have appeased the father with
a song, composed in honour of the deceased prince.

Note 28, page 35.

The traditions of Circassia mention a race of foreigners, who are generally supposed to have been wandering Crusaders. It is said that they erected those ancient castles, the ruins of which are still found in that country; and were, at length, expelled by the natives, whom they had oppressed.

Note 29, page 37.

Merem is adored, in Circassia, as a sort of goddess, supposed to preside over the harvest and bees. A feast is held, in her honour, at the autumnal equinox, accompanied with music and dancing.

Note 30, page 41.

Thunder and lightning, as they emanate from the great spirit Tkhâ, are regarded, by the Circassians, with great veneration; and happy is the man who is so distinguished as to fall a victim to their violence. His body is consigned to the earth, with much solemnity; and his family rejoice at the great honour conferred upon them.—*Spencer's Travels.*

Note 31, page 45.

The Circassians, in common with most nations, have a strong belief in dreams, as predictions of future events; and generally give names to their children according to the peculiar circumstances of their birth or personal appearance. Spencer says, that the Circassian for the stars is " Dizilé."

Note 32, page 47.

The manufacture of arms, and other arts which in Europe are considered peculiar to men, are said to be practised by ladies, even of the highest rank, in Circassia.

Note 33, page 47.

This signifies a teacher.

Note 34, page 52.

See Bell's account of the cure of the sick, in Circassia.

Note 35, page 54.

The worship of Merem is supposed to be a relic of ancient Christianity—and the goddess to be identical with the Virgin Mary. Amongst other ceremonies practised at her feast, are, dressing with garlands the ancient crosses already mentioned, and breaking bread, in every house, to procure the blessing of an abundant harvest.

Note 36, page 55.

A warlike princess of Imeretia; who is said to have converted the Caucasian tribes to Christianity,—but her proselytes were made chiefly by the sword.

Note 37, page 62.

Such offerings are said to be common, and held most sacred, in Circassia.

Note 38, page 66.

The Atalik is considered a second father to his Pkhûr, or pupil.

Note 39, page 71.

The Mamelukes called Napoleon Bonaparte—Sultaun Khebir, or Prince of Fire.

Note 40, page 81.

An eastern sage; who taught the doctrine of total annihilation, by death.

Note 41, page 85.

An isle near the coast of Circassia; so called, because tradition asserts that a great treasure is hidden there, but rendered inaccessible by the guardianship of an enormous serpent.

Note 42, page 86.

Nothing short of actual representation can convey an adequate idea of the impetuosity of a Circassian charge. To the very bravest European troops, it must be absolutely terrific; being executed, literally, with the rapidity of lightning—accompanied with a frightful war-cry, resembling the scream of the jackall.—*Spencer's Travels.*

Note 43, page 89.

See Spencer's Travels in Circassia.

Note 44, page 91.

The gipsies are known by this name, in Asia.

Note 45, page 97.

Soudjouk-Kalé is said to occupy the site of this ancient city.

MISCELLANEOUS POEMS.

PART I.

MISCELLANEOUS POEMS.

THE MAID OF THE RHONE.

" 'Twas in that lovely land, that lies
Where Alpine shadows fall
On scenes that, to the pilgrim's eyes,
Might Eden's bloom recall,—
As when, undimmed by curse or crime,
It rose amid the dawn of time,—
That early spring, whose blossoms grew
While yet the heavens and earth were new:
There, stood—beside the rapid Rhone,
That, now from Leman free,
By wood and city wall swept on,
To meet the classic sea—
An ancient and a stately hall,
With dungeon-keep and moated wall,
And battlements whose bannered pride
Had many a hostile host defied.

I

" And she, the lady of the tower,
Though last of all her line,
Was mightiest in the matchless power
Of beauty,—at whose shrine
The flower of chivalry adored,
And proved their vows by song and sword.
But knightly vow and minstrel strain
Beneath her lattice flowed in vain;
For, in the maiden's bower, there hung
A warrior's portrait—pale,
But wondrous beautiful and young,
And clad in burnished mail:
Oh! many an eye had marked it well,
But none that warrior's tale could tell,—
Save that he bore the Red Cross shield,
And fought in some far Syrian field.

" But there the maiden's earliest glance
And latest gaze would turn,
From thrilling harp and gleaming lance,
With love that seemed to spurn
All other vows, and serve alone
That nameless idol of its own.
For oft such glorious shadows rise,
And early hide from youthful eyes
The substance of this world, and claim
The heart's first-fruits, that taste
Of Paradise,—though nought but fame
Hath, on the altar, traced

The name no wave can wash away!—
As old remembered legends say,
The eastern maiden loved, so long,
The youth she only knew in song!

    " So loved the lady of the tower!
And summers glided on,
Till, one by one, from hall and bower,
Her kindred maids were gone;
Some had put on the bridal wreath,—
Some wore the chaplet twined for death:
But still no mortal charms could wean
Her fancy from that pictured mien.
At length, there came a noble knight,
Though past his manhood's prime;
His sword had been in many a fight,
His steps in many a clime:—
But ah! what thoughts that wooer's name
Awakened;—for it was the same
That the old painter's magic art
Had graven on the maiden's heart!

    " The idol of her youth was now
Before her! but she gazed
Upon the veteran's furrowed brow,—
And then, in wonder, raised
Her eyes to that bright pictured face,
Whose changeless beauty wore no trace

Of wasting time or withering war,
Like his, in furrow or in scar.
Oh! many a loved and lovely face,
Had grown less fond and fair,
Since first that picture met her gaze,
But, still, no change was *there!*
That age could dim or sorrow bow
The sunny cheek or stately brow—
She had not thought of things like these,
In all her lonely reveries!

   " Like him who saw, through Alpine woods,
The glacier's gem-like glow,
And climbed the rocks and crossed the floods,
To find it only snow,—
So felt the maiden—as she said:
' My star is set—my rainbow fled!
Why hast thou come at last,—to break
My pleasant dream?—how sad to wake!
What thoughts of thee, o'er heart and mind,
Have sped their visioned gleam :—
I meet thee, now—but not to find
The shadow of my dream!
This heart hath only bowed before
The glory that the canvass wore;
That spell hath past—my soul is free—
And turns no more to love—or thee!

" ' Go! find some fairer, happier bride,
Who hath not loved in vain;—
The light that in thy presence died,
May never shine again!
The passion that survived, in truth,
The roses and the smiles of youth,
Hath perished, like the pilgrim knight,
Who died, with Salem in his sight!'

*   *   *   *

" There is a cross on Sidon's shore,
That marks a Templar's rest;—
And cloister-arches darken o'er
A fairer, gentler guest.
So sleep the loving hearts, whom fate
Forbade to meet, till all too late;
And the same storied lands and waves
That parted them, divide their graves."

*   *   *   *

Thus sang the last of Troubadours,
Beneath the brightest eyes
That e'er looked forth from Harem bowers,
Upon the orient skies:—
And as he sang, the Caliph's bride,
Amid her eastern splendour, sighed,—
As if some secret sorrow then
Came up to memory's glance, again.

It might have been an early dream—
The tender and untold—
That years swept over, as the stream
Sweeps o'er the hidden gold
That sparkles brightly, through the sands
Of rivers, in the Indian lands!
And gold, and gems of dazzling sheen,
Were offered, by that eastern queen,
In vain;—" Then choose thine own reward,"
She said:—and, lo! the knightly bard
Pressed on her royal hand, that day,
His first, last kiss—and went his way!

LET US RETURN.

"Let us return!" said the broken heart
Of the mountain hermit's tale,—[1]
When he saw the morning mists depart
From the summits grey and pale:—
For he knew that the fan-palm cast the shade
Of its ever-glorious green
Where the love of his blasted youth was laid,
And the light of her steps had been.
Ah! thus, for ever, the heart looks back
To its young hope's funeral urn:—
To the tender green of that early track,
To its light, let us return!

The lines of our life may be smooth and strong,—
And our pleasant path may lie
Where the stream of affection flows along,
In the light of a summer sky:—
But woe for the lights that early wane,
And the shades that early fall,
And the prayer that speaks of the secret pain,
Though its voice be still and small!
To the sweeter flowers, to the brighter streams,
To the household hearths that burn

Still bright in our holy land of dreams,
To their love let us return!

'Tis well we have learned the truths of time,—
But they came with the winter's snow,
For we saw them not through the flowery prime
Of our summers long ago:
Yet the spring is green and the summer bright
As they were in the years of yore,
But on our souls the love and light
Of their gladness come no more!
Back—back to the wisdom of the years
That had yet no loss to mourn,—
To their faith, that found no place for tears,
To their joy, let us return!

We have paused, perchance, by the quiet grave
Of our young who early slept,—
And, since they left us, many a wave
O'er our weary bark hath swept;—
But, far in the morning light enshrined,
They gladden our backward gaze,
Or wake, like the breath of the summer's wind,
The soul of our better days.
Back—back! to the living wave, we drew,
With *them*, from a purer urn,—
To the path of the promise lost to view,
And its peace—let us return!

THE LAST SPRING.

"The spring is come!"—her steps are on our mountains!
I hear the waving of the ancient pines;
Solemn, but joyous, is the voice of fountains,
That murmur on, by old forsaken shrines.
Far in the woodlands early birds are singing,
Among the pleasant places where young flowers,
In silent sweetness, from the earth are springing,—
Their breathings fill the breeze, in twilight hours,
And reach me here, amid the city's hum,
Telling that spring is come!

"Oh! never seemed there winter days so dreary
As those that o'er my loneliness have past!
And I have waited, like a watcher weary,
For the first sunny smile—'tis come at last!
But many a glorious spring hath past and perished,
With all its greenness, from my native hills,
Where I have been a stranger; yet the cherished
Hope of the soul, which time nor tempest chills,
Hath borne me on, through clouds without a sun,—
And now the goal is won!

"The high place of my hopes!—and I have found it;
But ah! the temple is not what it seemed!
Where are the fadeless flowers that grew around it?
And where the quenchless stars that o'er it beamed?

Alas! the stars have fallen—the flowers have faded,
That seemed immortal, in my dreaming eyes,—
Even as the gardens of the desert, shaded
By trees whose verdure spoke of Paradise,
That lured the wanderer to the distant height,
Then faded from his sight!

"And such have been the heights of the world's glory
Which I have climbed;—ah! weary was the steep!
Amid whose glittering snows my heart grew hoary,
While summer breathed upon the valleys deep—
In vain—for none of all its roses won me,
From toiling upward to that mountain's brow:—
'Tis gained;—but ah! the weight of years is on me,—
My spirit cannot claim its birthright now!
For early that inheritance was sold,
For nought,—like his, of old!

" But yet, methinks, some dewdrops of my morning
Have lingered through the long and parching day;
I feel the childhood of my soul returning,
In visions of green forests, far away.
It is too late:—the cup hath past untasted,—
The noon was glorious, but I lost its glow;—
Oh! for but one of all the summers wasted!
And now the spring is come—but I must go
Where years their sunborn blossoms cannot bring:—
Farewell, thou blessed spring!"

THE PROMISED LAND.

———

"The rose hath past from my summer time,—
  For the lamp of life is low;
But I know there's hope in that better clime
  Where the healing waters flow:
I know there is life in the southern lands
  Where the sunshine knows no shade,—
For it lights the joy of the vintage bands,
  And the flowers that never fade.

"But I dreamed of a land, long—long ago,
  When my world of thought was new;
And *our* skies grew dim, in its brighter glow,
  And our roses lost their hue:—
For the glory of Eden's youth was there,
  Unseared by the soul's regret,
And the odours breathed through the blessed air,—
  They live in my spirit yet!

"Oh! long have I borne an exile's lot,
  And pined by my native streams;
For the light of that land was ne'er forgot,—
  It shone in my lonely dreams:

It shone in the spring-morn's early beam,
    In the summer's golden eves,
When the sky was bright with the day's last gleam,
    And the woods were dark with leaves.

" Ah! many a dream of my youth hath past,
    In its morning light, away,—
But the love of that bright land lingers last,
    On my early-closing day:
Oh! could I but reach its bowers, that bloom
    In their freshness ever fair!
For my steps are faint, in this wintry gloom,—
    But I know there's healing, there!

" My kindred joy in our northern night,
    When the stars shine coldly clear,
And the winds are low, and the hearths are bright,—
    But *my* heart's home is not here!"
Ah, lonely one! in thy vision's birth
    Was a glorious promise given;—
For well may there be no home on earth
    For the hearts that dream of heaven!

IN VAIN.

In vain!—how·many hearts are spent,
   And long years worn away,
And oh! how much to Hope is lent
   She never will repay!
For who can tell the toiling part,
   The waste of soul and brain,
The weary travel of the heart,
   Which have been borne—in vain!

The sleepless sage some star hath sought,
   Till hope and sight grew dim,—
It shone for eyes that loved it nought,
   But never looked on him:—
Thus fate hath flung the pearls away
   Which all was sold to gain,
Or freely poured the priceless ray
   Where it might shine—in vain!

The poet's song hath filled the earth
   By every sea and shore,
And shed around his land of birth
   A glory, evermore:—
But o'er the lyre hung clouds and gloom,
   Whence rose that matchless strain,
And the minstrel only found a tomb,
   With bright bays crowned—in vain!

The chief, whose name hath endless life—
  His country's trust and might—
Who found his fame, through days of strife
  And watchings of the night,—
Whose voice the powers of earth could shake,
  In senate, field or fane,—
Alas! and must the high hearts break,
  The faithful fall—in vain!

And love—the true, the pure—that clings,
  In spite of chill or rack,—
Oh! many give their precious things,
  But *it* kept nothing back:
Yet woe! for well-springs of the heart
  Poured unto dust like rain,
When world's-wealth could not purchase part
  Of what was given—in vain!

And some have borne the blast, unbowed,—
  But sunk beneath the wave,
When high the bow was in the cloud,
  Or life-boat near to save:—
Thus upon human skill and care
  Some blight will still remain;—
Then let us lay up treasures, where
  They are not heaped—in vain!

ALL THINGS NEW.

And He that sat upon the throne, said,
Behold! I make all things new.—REVELATION.

New Heavens!—for the stars grow pale,
  With the midnight scenes of time!
And the sun is weary of the wail
  That meets him in every clime;
And the sky grows dim with the mist of tears—
Bring back the blue of its first, bright years!

New Earth!—for the land and waves
  With a weight of evil groan;
And its dwellings stand on a soil of graves,
  Which fearful things hath known:—
From the touch of fire, from the battle-stain,
Give us its Eden green, again!

New Law!—for 'tis the arm of wrong,
  And great hath been the cry,
When oppressors' hands in their might grew strong,
  And their deeds have pierced the sky:—
But the powers are shaken;—oh! requite
With the free, unchanging law of right!

New Faith!—for a voice of blood
  Hath been heard from every shrine,
And the world hath worshipped many a God
  With rites it deemed divine:
But the creeds grow old and the fanes decay,—
Show us, at last, some better way!

New Hope!—for it rose among
  The thorns of a barren spot,
Where the bloom is brief and the labour long,
  And the harvest cometh not;—
And hearts grow weary that watch and wait,—
Give them a rainbow that fears not fate!

New Love!—for it hath been cast
  On the troubled waters, long,
And hoped in visions vain, that passed
  Away, like a nightbird's song:—
It may not be severed from the lost,
But give us the young world's love uncrossed!

New Life!—give the summers back
  Whose glory passed in vain,—
Redeem our days from the shadow black
  Of clouds without the rain,
And the wastes which bitter waters wore,—
And our canker-eaten years restore!

New Light!—for the lamps decay
   Which shone on the old world's youth,
And the wise man watches for a ray
   Of the undiscovered truth;—
Long hath he looked through the midnight dim,—
Let the glorious day-spring visit him!

Must the earth's last hope like a shadow flee?
   Was the dream of ages vain?
Oh! when will the bright restoring be,
   And the glory come again
Of our promised spring, with its blessed dew,—
And His word, that maketh all things new!

THE FIRST FRIEND.

The priceless gifts of the soul were his;
  And fame, whose early light
In darkness rose, as the stars arise
  From the silent depths of night:
And his upward course was brightly calm,—
For his glory grew like the fadeless palm;
It felt no blight and it feared no blast,
But stood in its greenness, to the last.

Yet ever around his spirit hung
  A shadow, like a spell,—
And his eye grew weary of looking long
  For a face remembered well:
Though many a bright one met his gaze,
In minster's gloom or in banquet's blaze,
Yet none could waken again the glow
That gladdened the pilgrim, long ago.

For, once, in the cold world's careless crowd,
  When hope was faint and dim,
Like a sunbeam bright through the wintry cloud,
  A young face smiled on him!

That moment seemed as if night were past,
And the day of his life had dawned at last;
And the strength of his soul returned again,
As rivers rise in the mountain rain.

Oh! never again could time or toil
   The wanderer tire or chill,
For he kept the light of that blessed smile—
   The star of his desert—still:
And now, he had reached the pleasant streams,—
But they took their hue from *its* quenchless beams;
For many shone on his after-lot,
But *that* was the only unforgot!

The winters passed, and the summers came,
   And his fortune's frowns were o'er,
For he wore the fadeless wreath of fame;—
   But he saw that face no more!
The sunny shore and the stormy sea,
The cities thronged and the woodlands free,
All—all he sought,—but he sought in vain,
For it never smiled on him again!

Oh! did the grave, in its quiet, close
   O'er the flower he loved so long,—
Whose nameless memory ever rose
   On the breath of his sweetest song?

Ah! many a lyre the laurel wreathes,
That but of the withered myrtle breathes,—
And the sweetest incense ever shed
Hath been an offering to the dead!

Silent and swift the years sped on,
  And they bore his youth away;
But the vision lingered still, that shone
  So bright on his early day:
For roses fade, when the summer flies,—
But the rose of the canvass never dies!
And thus, when his summer days were gone,
The rose of his memory still bloomed on.

Oh! well that he had not seen it fade,
  Or change as the living changed,—
But blooming ever, through sun and shade,
  In its beauty unestranged!
There fell no blight on its tearless youth,—
There came no stain on his spirit's truth;—
For he sought that friend on the earth no more,
But turned his gaze to a brighter shore!

THE PARTING GIFTS.

'Twas early spring; and the violet's scent
The winds from the woodlands bore,—
Where stood a youth, on far travel bent,
At a lonely cottage door.
His best beloved stood with him there:
One was a sister young and fair,
With eyes of azure and golden hair,
And the rose-bud's early bloom,—
The other had locks like raven wings,
And her dark eye showed thought's deeper springs,—
For she seemed as if born for higher things
Than a peasant's hearth or tomb;
But dearer far to that youth was she
Than sister, country or home could be.

And yet, he went—for their lowly lot
Was darkened by fortune's frown,
That brings a blight on the peasant's cot,
As well as the monarch's crown:—
But, ere they parted, that dark-eyed maid
Gave, from her brow, one raven braid—
Ah! long had the peasant-lover prayed
For that shining tress in vain!
But it was given freely now
As the golden curl from his sister's brow,

With many a blessing and many a vow,
And the hope to meet again.
So he turned away from the cottage door,
With tears he went—but he came no more!

Long years had passed; and the northern night,
In its starry splendour, shone
On a stately chamber, hushed and bright,
Where an old man sat alone.
He sat alone, by a silent hearth,
That knew no music of household mirth!
And far from the country of his birth
Was the wanderer's dwelling now:
His eyes were dim, and his locks were gray,—
Yet oft would his lonely visions stray
To a woodland cottage far away,
And a maiden's whispered vow!
For the boy who had left his home with tears,
Was the same with that man of fame and years.

Oh! bright did the star of his fortune beam,
In a far and stranger clime;
But he lost the light of his early dream,
And the flowers of his summer time!
He had stood in the sceptre's shade of power,—
He had shone in the senate's thoughtful hour,—
Through the battle field and the festive bower
The path of his fame had past;

But age was with him, and nought remained
Of all that his toil and years had gained,
To which he turned with a love unfeigned
And changeless to the last,—
Save the golden curl and the raven braid,
And the looks from memory ne'er to fade!

How fondly, still, were the tokens saved
Of that early parting scene,—
When the grass was long, and the wild weeds waved,
Where the cottage hearth had been,—
And the light of the golden locks was low,—
For the dust had covered them, long ago!
And the queen of his early joy or woe,
Her fortunes, too, were changed;
For she kept youth's pledge, to woman grown,
And a more than regal wreath put on,—
But the dark hair's glory, long, was gone,
And the lovers far estranged:—
Yet time brought neither snow nor shade
On the golden curl and the raven braid!

And now, as the old man gazed on them,
How the tide of time rolled back,
Till the years of his youth before him came,
Like a green untrodden track!
The hope that was then his only store,
And the love that had been his early lore,

And the home that should smile for him no more,
To his weary heart returned!
Ambition's dream had been more than crowned,—
And his age a fairer home had found,—
But the light of the love that had shone around
His youth, he missed and mourned:—
And pomp looked pale, in the mystic shade
Of the golden curl and the raven braid!

Ah! well might the Persian Vizier prize
The weeds of his shepherd-years,
That brought again to his aged eyes
The dew of his childhood's tears!
And thus had that old man prized and kept
The tokens frail of the love that slept
Too long—till time had darkly swept
Its fairest flowers away!
By strangers laid, at length, to rest,
Strange hands arranged, upon his breast,
The locks his dying fingers prest,
When their clasp was turned to clay:—
But they knew not the wealth of affection laid
With the golden curl and the raven braid!

THE PICTURE OF THE DEAD.

SUGGESTED BY AN ANECDOTE IN CATLIN'S TRAVELS.

A chief from his distant forest came,
　　To the pale one's lonely tent;
And he brought such gifts as a prince might claim,
　　By an Indian monarch sent:—
And " Bright may the sun on thy dwelling shine!"
　　Said the warrior of the wild,—
" Stranger, the gifts I bear are thine,
　　Who hast given me back my child!

" My child, who passed to the spirit-land,
　　In the sunrise of her years:—
I have looked for her in our woodland band,
　　Till mine eyes grew dim with tears:
But her shadow bright, by thy pencil traced,
　　Still sweet in my dwelling smiled,
And the hearth she left is not yet a waste,—
　　Thou hast given me back my child!

" I laid her low, in the place of graves,
　　Where the ever-silent slept;
And summer's grass, in its greenness, waves
　　Where an Indian warrior wept:—

For bright was our star, that early set,
　Till we lost its lustre mild;
But she lives in her changeless beauty yet,—
　Thou hast given me back my child!

" And say! when our young, who loved her well,
　Like the pines grow old and hoar,
Will her youth still last, as theirs that dwell
　Where the winter comes no more?
When the early loved of her heart is low,
　Will she smile as she ever smiled?
Oh! safe from the withering hand of woe,
　Hast thou given me back my child!

" 'Tis well with those of thine eastern land;
　Though their loved ones may depart,
The magic power of the painter's hand
　Restores them to the heart.
Oh! long may the light of *their* presence stay,
　Whose love *thy* griefs beguiled!
And blessings brighten thy homeward way,—
　Who hast given me back my child!"

STREAMS.

Ye early minstrels of the earth,—
  Whose mighty voices woke
The echoes of its infant woods,
  Ere yet the tempest spoke!
How is it, that ye waken still
  The young heart's happy dreams,
And shed your light on darkened days,
  O bright and blessed streams!

Woe for the world!—she hath grown old
  And grey, in toil and tears;—
But ye have kept the harmonies
  Of her unfallen years:
For ever, in our weary path,
  Your ceaseless music seems
The spirit of her perished youth,—
  Ye glad and glorious streams!

Your murmurs bring the pleasant breath
  Of many a sylvan scene,—
They tell of sweet and sunny vales,
  And woodlands wildly green.
Ye cheer the lonely heart of age,—
  Ye fill the exile's dreams
With hope and home and memory,—
  Ye unforgotten streams!

Too soon the blessed springs of love
    To bitter fountains turn,
And deserts drink the stream that flows
    From hope's exhaustless urn;
And faint, upon the waves of life,
    May fall the summer beams,—
But they linger long and bright with you,
    Ye sweet unchanging streams!

The bards—the ancient bards—who sang
    When thought and song were new,
O, mighty waters! did they learn
    Their minstrelsy from you?
For still, methinks, your voices blend
    With all their glorious themes,
That flow for ever, fresh and free
    As the eternal streams!

Well might the sainted seer, of old,
    Who trod the tearless shore,
Like many waters deem the voice
    The angel hosts adore!
For still, where deep the rivers roll,
    Or far the torrent gleams,
Our spirits hear the voice of God,
    Amid the rush of streams!

THE FIRST AND LAST SMILE.

Too fair she seemed for our fading earth;
But sorrow had darkened her hour of birth,
And tears on her cradle rest were shed,—
For she was a child of the early dead.
Yet fair she grew, as the forest flowers
That blossom in lands more bright than ours,—
As palms that rise in the eastern wild,
The girl was fair—but she never smiled!

And yet, no sorrow might dim the light
Of eyes that glistened so darkly bright;
But they were full of sleepless thought,—
As if the soul, in its silence, sought
Some path to its kindred stars, that lay,
In their lonely brightness, far away!
'Twas sad to look on a blooming child,
Who knew not sorrow—yet never smiled!

Early she loved the storied page,
And sought the treasures of bard and sage,
And early bent on the earth and skies
The searching gaze of her earnest eyes:

But she lingered not where the joyous crowd
Of young hearts revelled in laughter loud,—
For dearer far were the woodlands wild,
But even on their flowers she never smiled!

The mother watched o'er her passing years,
That came and went without smiles or tears,
As Parsees gaze on the circling sun,—
For she was her first and only one:
Swiftly her childhood passed away,
And youth came, bright as a summer's day,—
For charms that many a heart beguiled
Were showered on her—but she never smiled!

Vain prayers were poured for her heart and hand,
By princely youths of her native land;
But it seemed that the maiden's hope and trust
Were not in the dying things of dust,
And her lonely spirit had risen above
The golden fetters of earthly love.
She looked on *one* with a sadness mild,—
But on friend or lover—she never smiled!

At length, like a blighting blast, there came
A swift decay o'er her gentle frame,—
For the rose of our valleys lost her bloom,
And we knew she was chosen for the tomb!

The mother looked on her fading flower,
With hope that lived to the latest hour,—
Till the spell was broken that bound the past,—
In death the maiden—smiled at last!

And well was the mother's heart repaid
For all the love with her lost one laid,
By the truths that spoke in that dying gaze,
Thus lighted up to a moment's blaze:—
The hoarded smiles of a life were there,
Undimmed by time and unblanched by care,—
And the shadows of earth could ne'er defile
The joy of that first—and latest—smile!

DREAMS OF THE DEAD.

The peasant dreams of lowly love,—
　　The prince of courtly bowers,—
And exiles, through the midnight, rove
　　Among their native flowers:—
But flowers depart, and, sere and chill,
　　The autumn leaves are shed,
And roses come again—yet still,
　　My dreams are of the dead!

The voices in my slumbering ear
　　Have woke the world, of old,—
The forms that in my dreams appear
　　Have mingled with the mould;
Yet still they rise around my rest,
　　In all their peerless prime,—
The names by new-born nations blest—
　　The stars of elder time!

They come from old and sacred piles,
　　Where glory's ashes sleep,—
From far and long-deserted aisles,—
　　From desert or from deep,—

From lands of ever-verdant bowers,
   Unstained by mortal tread;—
Why haunt ye thus my midnight hours,
   Ye far and famous dead?

I have not walked with *you*, on earth,—
   My path is lone and low,—
A vale where laurels have not birth,
   Nor classic waters flow:
But on the sunrise of my soul
   Your mighty shades were cast,
As cloud-waves o'er the morning roll,—
   Bright children of the past!

And oft, with midnight, I have met
   The early wise and brave,—
Oh, ever great and glorious, yet,
   As if there were no grave!
As if, upon their path of dust,
   Had been no trace of tears,
No blighted faith, no broken trust,
   Nor waste of weary years!

But ah! *my* loved of early days,—
   How brightly still they bring
Upon my spirit's backward gaze
   The glory of its spring!

L

The hopes that shared their timeless doom
　　Return, as freshly green
As though the portals of the tomb
　　Had never closed between!

Oh! man may climb the mountain snows,
　　Or search the ocean wave,—
But who will choose to walk with those
　　Whose dwelling is the grave?—
Yet, when upon that tideless shore
　　His sweetest flowers are shed,
The lonely dreamer shrinks no more
　　From visions of the dead!

NOTES

Note 1, page 119.

Paul and Virginia.

Note 2, p. 121.

These were the last words of Goethe.

THE

VISION OF SCHWARTZ.

Muse of the dark and dreamy days
Whose clouds return no more,—
Whose harp hath kept the mystic lays
Of long forgotten lore!
Who read'st the magic, writ, in light,
Upon the desert sky,
And saw'st the Alchemist, by night,
His lonely labours ply,
With still-untiring hope, that ne'er
Was dimmed by time or chilled by fear!

Whence shall we call thee!—Is thy road
Through Danube's woods of pine,—
Or where the ruins look abroad,
Upon the rushing Rhine?
Or sleeps thy silent harp-string, hid
In some Crusader's tomb,—
Where knightly banners fade, amid
The minster's solemn gloom,—

His only fitting place of rest
Who hath the red-cross on his breast!

Whate'er thy name, whate'er thy clime,—
From fane or turret hoar,
O, spirit of the ancient time!
Lift up thy voice once more!
Sing of the visions fancy-nurst,
That rose, in times afar,
For that lone man who forged, at first,[1]
The thunderbolts of war,
And gave to death a dart more keen
Than all its early shafts had been!

    *   *   *   *

The watcher's wasted lamp was dim,
As early day drew nigh,—
But all unfelt, unmarked by him,
The silent hours sped by:
For his were vigils long and lone,
And labours shared or soothed by none,—
Nor friendly hand nor gentle tone
Might ever reach him there;
Where, far concealed from passing gaze,
And lit by faint and fitful blaze,
A cell—perchance, in other days,
The scene of secret prayer—
A vaulted dungeon, saw the toil
He wasted o'er the midnight oil.

Night was around; but deeper night
Upon the nations hung—
Night where no planet shed its light,
Nor meteor lamp was flung:
The stars of Greece had left her shore,—
Where even their memory was no more;
And Rome the mystic mantle wore
That all her glory veiled;
The Nine by Castaly had wept,
Till, wearied by their tears, they slept,—
All save Calliope, who kept
The fount—but kept it sealed,
Till Dante trod its marge,—and then,
The blessed waters flowed again!

Night hung upon the nations, dark
As earth had ever seen;
Yet shone, at times, some glimmering spark,
Where ancient fires had been;—
But, lost in deserts far away,—
Like comet from its course astray,—
It shed a faint uncertain ray,
That lit but could not guide,—
Or only lured the wanderer on,
To wider wilds—and then was gone!
And if the light of coming dawn
Far distant he descried,
'Twas through the glare of burnished brands,
And faggots piled by priestly hands!

Yet, on that night, what fancies smiled,—
The false, the brightly vain!
How many an untold vision wild,
Of glory or of gain,
Rose on the lonely student's hours,
By cottage hearth or courtly bowers,
Or where the convent's holy towers
And cloister-hidden cells
Shut out the world's wild vanities!
How bright they sparkled in those eyes
That turned to Heaven, and could despise
Young beauty's potent spells!—
And such was he who watched, that night,
Beside the lone fire's hidden light.

There was no furrow on his brow,
Nor whiteness in his hair,—
And yet it seemed that ages now
Could work no ruin there;
For youth and hope and passion's trace,
If ever there they had their place,
Had early vanished from his face,
And left it coldly calm,—
Like Lebanon's old crown of snow,
Unmoved by storm or summer's glow,
As he had seen it, long ago,
Beneath the Syrian palm:
But in his eye there lingered yet
The brightness of a glory set.

Was it the stone of power he sought?
Was it the draught of life?
The idols of the old world's thought,
Through Cross and Crescent's strife,—
For which her thousands toiled, like him,
Till life and all its lights grew dim;
Still, when their cup was to the brim,
And hope was all but crowned,
Some unseen hand would quench her beam,
And smite the image of her dream,
And leave it like that fabled stream,[2]—
The sought but never found!
Ah! ever thus her hopes have gone,—
And yet, the weary world hopes on!

But now, whate'er that silent one
Had sought, through perils past,
The labour of his life was done,—
The treasure found, at last!
And marble-like the chemist stands,
Time's glasses in his wasted hands,
With eye that counts the measured sands
Which ebb so slowly true:—
Another hour, he shall have gained
The height at which his spirit strained,—
The strife be o'er, the goal attained—
The prize is full in view!
Yet after-life shall want the power
To pay for that one burning hour!

It passed as many an hour hath past
Since Adam's dreary fall—
Ah! lavished with a spendthrift's waste,
And soon beyond recall!—
But ere its latest voice was past,
A sound, like winter's echoing blast,
Or ocean's booming, deep and vast,
Upon the midnight came!
The awful thunder with it blent,
And far and fearful sounds were sent,—
The crash of fallen battlement,
And roar of rushing flame—
A din, as of some distant world,
Amid the stars, to ruin hurled!

The trembling chemist stood amazed,—
Till ceased the storm of sound;
Yet high and bright his furnace blazed,
And o'er the vessel's round
There shone a blue and boding light,
That shook his very soul with fright,—
Such show had never met his sight,
Amid his art, before!
And stronger still his terror grew,
When sank the flame, with sulphur hue;
Yet, by its light, he bent to view
His now transmuted store:—
Ah! what repays his toil and trust?—
A heap of dim, discoloured dust!

It seemed the very dust of hell!—
The ashes of that fire
That ever burns, unquenchable
As the Eternal's ire!—
Or upcast of the burning deep,
Flung out from Hecla's snowy steep,
Upon the glacier's wintry sleep,
Amid the icy isle!—
Thick sulphurous vapours filled the cell,
Like those which, Parsee pilgrims tell,
Arise from Shirran's burning well![3]
The chemist paused, awhile;
And doubts came darkly o'er his heart,—
Was this the end of all his art?

In wrath and fear the monk essayed
To fling the dust away;
When lo! his lifted hand was stayed!
And by the waning ray,
He saw beside his furnace stand
A sage of the far eastern land,—
With flowing robe and snowy wand,
And mild majestic air!
The features he had seen, before,
Upon Arabia's desert shore,—
But yet the majesty it wore
No face of man might wear;—
For beauty to the brow was given,
Too bright for earth, too dark for heaven!

Saw he a form of mortal mould,
Amid the dying gleam?
Or one the slumbering world, of old,
Beheld in many a dream,—
Who walked in solitude sublime,
Among the tribes of every clime,
And feared not death, and felt not time,
In his unfading youth,—
For still the brightness of his eye
Seemed kindled for eternity,
And yet it was not of the sky?—
The monk was awed, in sooth;
Yet were it spirit, sage or seer,
He bowed in reverence more than fear.

" Child of a dying race!" began
That uninvited guest,—
(Oh! never had the voice of man
Such power to pierce the breast!)—
" Child of a dying race!—whose years
May dawn in hope, but close in fears,—
Who faintly mark their path with tears,
And then like shadows flee,—
Yet, in their darkened wanderings, still,
The changeless laws of fate fulfil,
And ope the founts of good and ill,—
Nor in their waters see
The future rivers, waves and sands,—
Behold the work of thine own hands!"

He said;—and waved his mystic wand:
The friar in silence gazed,—
And lo! before that mighty hand,
The convent-walls seemed razed
To their foundations!   Far and wide,
The prospect spread on every side,
Where summer left no cloud, to hide
Roumelia's blooming bowers;—
As rose upon his raptured eyes
The light of Europe's eastern skies,
And, by its sea of gem-like dyes,
Byzantium's sacred towers,—
That, in their grandeur lone, seemed all
Of ancient empire left to fall!

   Still fair, between her meeting seas,
The stately city stood,—
The bulwark and the crown of Greece,—
A queen in solitude!
A dying queen—for, at her gate,
Behold the Moslem legions wait
The hour that makes her desolate,
And lays her glory low!
Venice! what ocean-storms have met
Thy galleys, that they come not yet?
And can the Templar's sword forget
To strike the avenging blow?
The cry is long and loud and deep,—
But deeper still the nations sleep!

O, last of Greece! thine hour is near!—
From Asia's deserts far,
Thy spoilers come, with bow and spear,
With horse and scimitar!
Yet still, though arts and arms assail,
The long-forsaken Greeks prevail,—
And oft the Paynim thousands quail
Before their deep despair:—
But lo! what sons of war are these,⁴
That speak in thunder?—On the breeze
Their clouds ascend,—and Europe sees
Their ceaseless lightnings glare,—
And rocks they fling, of monstrous mould,
As those by Titans cast, of old!

No longer may the Grecian walls
Withstand that fearful shock,—
The barrier yields, the rampart falls,
Before the flying rock.
She falls, with all her faithful spears—
The home of sages, bards and seers—
The child of Athens' brightest years,⁵
The heir of conquering Rome;
She falls—old Asia's royal bride,
Who foiled so many a conqueror's pride!⁶
And must the boundless Tartar-tide
Above her splendours foam?
Wide o'er her sweeps the Moslem's wrath,
And blood and ruin mark his path!

Yet still, a dying glory gleams
Around the city's fall,
That, in her latest moment, seems,
Though faintly, to recall
The sword of her first Constantine;—
Thou, last and noblest of his line!'
Could fate no better doom assign
To one so wisely brave?
Then go, with thy worn crown!—till now,
'Twas but a shadow on thy brow!
Oh! long thy land's last laurel bough
Shall flourish on thy grave,—
For thou hast perished, as became
The bearer of a conquering name!

Far floats the crescent on the air,
And peals the Othman's joy:—
"But say, what viewless power was there,
So mighty to destroy?
From what Cyclopean furnace came
The winged rocks and bolts of flame,
That smote, with such a deadly aim,
Byzantium's iron strength?
Or did the earth, in fear and pain,
Bring forth her Titan sons again,
To prove our human efforts vain?"
So spake the friar, at length:—
But silently the wand waved on,
And scene and city—all were gone!

Then slowly rose upon his view
A strange and distant shore,—
A land where nature's self was new,
A world unknown before!
Full many a land the monk had seen,
And far his pilgrim-steps had been,
Through desert sands and forests green,
And cities old in fame;—
Where rose the Nile's eternal fanes,
Where spread Zahara's burning plains,
And where the north, with icy chains,
Made the wild rivers tame;
But nought on earth's remotest strand
Could match the wonders of that land.

The steeps of heaven its mountains seemed,
Its plains unruffled seas;
And never through its forests streamed
The sunbeam or the breeze.
Mighty and deep its rivers rolled,
Like infant oceans, sprung of old
From the great deluge,—gems and gold
Were gleaming through their waves,—
Perchance the wealth that once went down,
With buried nations of renown,
And many a long forgotten crown!
Why had the ancient graves
Cast up their hidden stores, again,
To tempt a flood of redder rain?

Ah, land of gold! destruction lies
In thine exhaustless mines;
The fires that fright thy cloudless skies,—
The blood that stains thy shrines,—
Thy bold invader's conquering sword,—
And that yet unforgotten horde
Upon thine after ages poured,
The bearded buccaneers,—
Were offspring of the fatal dower
Bequeathed thee, in a luckless hour;
To other lands the spring of power,
To thee the fount of tears,—
A fountain that, in all but hope,
Might with Pandora's coffer cope!

World of the West! say, was't for thee,
The Cambrian* left his hills,—
Where, still, his dream-like memory
The mountain legend fills?
Was it the waving of thy woods,—
Was it the thunder of thy floods,
O'er ocean's trackless solitudes
By western breezes borne,
That reached the lone Athenian sage,
Who glorified the Grecian page
With visions of a golden age,
And blessed isles, unworn
By weary feet—unwet by tears,
And crowned with ever cloudless years?*

M

Whence came those glorious shadows?—Say,
Ye far and nameless tombs!
Ye silent cities, lost to day
Amid the forest glooms!
Is there no echo in the glades,
Whose massive foliage never fades,—
No voice among the pathless shades,
To tell of glory gone?
Gone from faint memory's fading dreams,
From shepherd's tales and poet's themes;
And yet the bright, eternal streams
Unwasted still roll on,—
Majestic as they rolled, before
A sail had sought, or found, the shore.

But by those mighty rivers, *then*,
What peaceful nations met,
Among the race of mortal men
Unnamed, unnumbered yet!
And cities rose and temples shone,
And power and splendour graced the throne,
And autumn's riches, freely strown,
Repaid the peasant's pains;
For homes of love and shrines of prayer
And fields of storied fame were there,
And smiling landscapes freshly fair—
The haunts of happy swains,—
And many a wide and trackless wild,
Where roved the forest's tameless child.

Ah! brightly bent the southern heaven
O'er woodland wave and glen;—
For to that gazer's sight was given
The eagle's piercing ken.
But hark! a sudden sound of fear!
The foe, the stranger foe, is near!
The Inca grasps his golden spear,
And calls his warrior bands:
And now, from many a mountain peak,
From many a lake that islands streak,
Behold the swarthy legions break,
And draw their battle brands,
For all by faith or hope endeared,—
Their homes beloved—their gods revered!

Shades of Columbia's perished host!
How shall a stranger tell
The deeds that glorified your coast,
Before its warriors fell?
Where sleeps thy mountain muse, Peru?
And Chili's matchless hills of dew,
Had they no harp, to freedom true,
No bard of native fire,
To sing his country's ancient fame,
And keep the brightness of her name
Unfading as the worshipped flame?—
The wealth of such a lyre
Outvalues all the blood-bought ore
That e'er Iberia's galleons bore.

Iberia! on thine ancient crown
The blood of nations lies,
With power to weigh thy glory down,—
With voice to pierce the skies!
For written with an iron pen,
Upon the memories of men,
The deeds that marked thy conquest, then,
For evermore remain :—
And still the saddest of the tale
Is Afric's wild and weary wail,—
Though prelates spread the slaver's sail,[10]
And forged the negro's chain:
The curse of trampled liberty
For ever clings to thine and thee!

Well may the old volcanoes cast
Their ashes on thy path,
Till cities wither in the blast
Of Chimborazo's wrath!
Avenger of a ruined race,
From whose deserted dwelling-place
No passing summers can efface
The memory of their wrong!
And though fair freedom's image shine,
At times, beside her ruined shrine,—
'Tis such an idol, deemed divine,
And worshipped by the throng,
As when the demon-prince put on
The regal robes of Solomon![11]

Bright were the spears and brave the hearts
That held those early fields,—
And vain, against their poisoned darts,
Were Europe's knightly shields.
But say, is that the lightning's flash,
That smites the warriors, as they dash
Upon their foes?—The mountain ash
Ne'er shed its shrivelled leaves
So fast, before the winter's breath,
As fall their crowds, by hill and heath,
Where fast the ancient reaper, Death,
Mows down the mortal sheaves!
For still, where nations win or yield,
Death is the victor of the field!

They fall as fell the perished brave
For whom no wreaths have sprung,
Who sank in silence to the grave
Unstoried and unsung.
In vain Peru renews her darts,—
In vain La Plata plies her arts,—
And Chili[12] sends her dauntless hearts,
That would not bow, but bleed.
Ah! wherefore fails the righteous cause?
Oh! must the sword that freedom draws,
When arming for her holiest laws,
Be found a broken reed?
Woe for the nations!—it was so
With Montezuma's Mexico!

On sweeps the ruthless conqueror's power,
Resistless in its course!
He tracks the savage to his bower,
The river to its source:
Before his march, the landscape lies
Like Adam's early paradise,—
When dimly loured upon its skies
The shadow of the curse;
But far behind him, deserts spread,
With ruined cities and their dead,—
A land whence life and hope are fled—
A wilderness—or worse,
As surely as the land of slaves
Is sadder than the place of graves!

On sweeps the conqueror!—and the gold
Of empires strews his track;
But never did the muse unfold
A tale so foully black!
The bard disdains, and sages shun,
To tell the deeds that there were done,
Before the blessed stars and sun,
For that accursed dross.—
But who can paint the thoughts that roll
Like billows o'er the friar's soul,
As he beholds the sacred stole
And ever-saving cross
Lead on the wars, whose very name
Should redden Europe's cheek with shame!

In mortal horror, more than rage,
He turned him from the sight,
To where that ever-silent sage,
With eye so calmly bright,
Stood gazing on the wasted land,—
As though the wonders of his wand
Were truths in storied pages scanned,
Since childhood's early day.
And—"Father! say, what power unblest
Hath been that region's fatal guest,
And swept the nations of the west,
With all their hopes, away?"
He asked:—but dim in distance grew
The scene, and faded from his view!

On waved the wand:—and, at his feet,
Far flowed the sleepless sea;
And o'er it rode a gallant fleet,
Like eagles proudly free!
They bore the banners of the brave,
Who seek dominion on the wave,
Nor feel that ocean, like the grave,
No human sceptre owns;—
For restless rolls the mighty main,
As when it mocked the Persian's chain,—[13]
Or taught the wisely-royal Dane[14]
That lesson, by the thrones
So soon forgot—so oft renewed
By earth's o'erburthened multitude.

Afar, upon that fading sky,
In distant whiteness, rose
The sails that met the watcher's eye,
And told of ocean-foes.
As o'er the waters, vast and dark,
Came towering on each giant bark,
With life o'erflowing, as the ark—
But ah! without the dove!—
Unlike the sails of Venice old,
Or prows of which Greek tale hath told,—
With freer course and port more bold,
The mighty strangers move;
But well the gazing friar knew
Their waving cross, of sanguine hue!

On deadly deeds of battle bent,
The hostile squadrons meet,—
For all a nation's hate was sent,
With each adventurer's fleet.
They met: but never thunder spoke
So dread as o'er that meeting broke;
And many a sea-born echo woke,
In caverns vast and deep;
And ne'er had midnight's wintry cloud
The blackness of the sulphurous shroud,
Through which their fiery arrows ploughed,
And glared on wave and steep,—
Such sudden bursts of lurid light
As flash, in Etna's hour of might!

The friar had been upon the deep,
When waves were high and wild,
And midnight winds could banish sleep
From ocean's sternest child;
And he had seen the billows march
Spanned by the lightning's fiery arch,
Whose living brightness seemed to search
The sinner's soul;—his ear
Had caught the thunder's dreadful hail
Roll mingling with the tempest's wail,
When bowed the mast before the gale,
No hope nor helper near;—
But nought, on earth, or sea, or air,
That matched the tempest raging there!

And now the battle's dingy veil
Was lifted by the breeze,
Where proudly rode the stranger-sail,
As victors of the seas:—
Few—few were they, whose path had been
So stately ere those sails were seen;
But each seemed yet an ocean queen,
Though only three remained.
One, like a furnace blazing far,
Appeared the very shrine of war,
Lit up for sacrifice—a star
That fell, but never waned.
And with its voice of fire, were sent
Such sounds as pierce the firmament.

Another was a stately bark,
And bore a gallant crew;
And high above the towering ark
Their rainbow-banner flew.
But lo! unsmote by sword or flame,
A moment reeled the mighty frame,—
Then sank, with all her sons of fame!
And, mid the waters' close,
Burst out one wild inspiring cheer,
Never to reach their country's ear;—
And mingling with it, sweet and clear,
An infant voice arose,
While latest, o'er the billows, smiled
The sunny face of that fair child!

The last had borne the battle's brunt,
And seemed a floating tower,
That bore, upon its awful front,
The frown of fearless power.
Sudden, with deep unearthly sound,
The giant takes an upward bound,
Then bursts in air, and far around
Descends the fearful rain,—
A rain of ruin, blent with fire,
As if the old Olympian Sire
Had scattered lightning, in his ire!—
Then waved the wand, again,—
And conquering fleet and sea and shore
Were lost to sight—and all was o'er!

The friar surveyed his silent cell,
Like one from dreams awoke;
Then, solemn as the night-wind's swell,
That nameless prophet spoke:—
" Lone dreamer of a day! for thee,
The ever-barred futurity
Hath flung her portals wide and free;
The pierceless clouds of time
Were rent before thee,—and thy gaze
Hath dwelt on deeds of distant days,
That yet shall mingle in the maze
Of human woe and crime!
Thy search is past—thy labour o'er—
And fate demands of thee no more!

" But worse than all thine eyes have seen
Earth's coming years shall see;—
Ah! little do its warriors ween
The power that sleeps with thee!
A power to scatter far and wide,
On desert wind or ocean tide,
The city's wealth, the galley's pride,
Wherein the nations trust.
Sons of the stately chivalry!
Go, fling the brazen buckler by,
And yield the knightly panoply
To time's corroding rust!
For helm of proof and iron mail,
The matchless once, no more avail.

" Still, in her pride, Constantia[15] stands,
With all her stately towers!
The billows bear, to Europe's sands,
The yet unnoticed flowers[16]
That speak of far and lovely isles,
And lands where cloudless summer smiles
On peopled plains and stately piles
And old imperial thrones!
But *this* shall stain the brightest wave,—
Shall sweep those empires to the grave,—
And heap, in many a mountain cave,
The Carrib's whitening bones;—[17]
And bid the eastern crescent shine
Above Sophia's sainted shrine!"

" And is it thus repaid, at last—
My weary search for truth?
Was it for this my spirit cast
Away her glorious youth,
And made her roses early sere?
For human love and human fear,
And all the ties that bind us here,
Her higher hopes have spurned,—
And spent her spring in thankless toil,
Upon a bleak and barren soil,—
Whose fruit, when found, like Timour's[18] spoil,
To dust and ashes turned,—
Ashes, that more of ill contain
Than all Gomorrah's fiery rain?

"O! master of the hidden lore,
Whose dark revealings, now,
Shall haunt my slumbers, evermore,—
From whence, and what, art thou?"
The chemist ceased—for on his cell
A moment's twilight shadow fell,
As soft as on the dewy dell
Descends the eve of June;
And the deep curfew, far remote,
Blent with the night-bird's lonely note,
Upon the still air seemed to float,
In sweet and solemn tune!
And when the song and shadow flew,
The prophet-guest had vanished, too!

The chemist was alone, again,
Beside his waning light;
But never in his soul did wane
The memory of that night.
Still, dim before him lay the dust,
That seemed destruction's future trust:—
" And is it thus," he cried,—"and must
The world be cursed by me?
Ah! rather, since an endless spring
Of death is in this lifeless thing,
Let me the fatal ashes fling
On waters wild and free,—
And ne'er, to human eye or ear,
Make known its mystery of fear!"

He started!—in his fading flame
Was stirred each dying brand,
As sudden from the embers came
A black nnguided hand,—
That wrenched, with fierce and fiery grasp,
The ashes from the chemist's clasp!—
Oh! ne'er had Afric's deadly asp
Such power of mortal pain,
As shot, that moment, like the dart
Of lightning, to his stricken heart,
And left—beyond his reach of art—
A long-abiding stain,[19]
That lingered to his close of life—
The badge of that unearthly strife!

His soul grew sick with mortal fear,
As loud the convent bell
Pealed forth, upon his startled ear,
What seemed a funeral knell!
The slumbering brothers, one and all,—
The warder on the castle wall,—
The guests amid the festive hall,—
In terror heard the sound;
And many a peasant rose to pray—
And lonely traveller longed for day—
As deep its echoes died away,
Among the wilds around!—

But long the legend of that hour
Remained, alike in hall and bower.

*   *   *   *

'Tis said, that, far in Albion's isle,
Beside a druid stone,
To mark the morning's early smile,
A watcher sat, alone:—
And, where the yellow sunset gleamed
On far Cathay,[20] and brightly streamed
Along the wondrous wall, that seemed
A mound of burnished gold,—
Marking the west, a dreamer stood,
Beside an ancient altar, rude
And ruined in its solitude,
Where-giant men of old,
Long ere Confucius saw the light,
Poured offerings to the god of night.

Lonely they watched—and far apart
As mortal men may be—
The hour whose gift should crown their art
Of might and mystery.
The sunset faded from the rills
Whose path the breeze Siberian chills;—
And bright on Albion's heathy hills,
Arose the summer morn:—

And morn and eve, and day and night,
Sped onward, in their ceaseless flight;
But bard knows not, nor sage can write,
To *which* that gift was borne!—
Ah! well its deadly work is done,
In cities lost or battles won!

NOTES

TO THE VISION OF SCHWARTZ.

Note 1, page 150.

Berthold Schwartz, a monk, who lived about the beginning of the twelfth century, is said to have discovered the art of making gunpowder, in his search for the philosopher's stone.

Note 2, page 153.

The stream whose waters were said to confer immortal youth.

Note 3, page 155.

The burning well of Shirran is a spring of naphtha,—said to have burned since the creation.

Note 4, page 158.

Mohammed II. is said to have employed, at the siege of Constantinople, the first pieces of cannon ever seen in Europe; from which were thrown balls, of immense size, made of a kind of stone, brought from the Euxine.

Note 5, page 158.

Byzantium (afterwards Constantinople) was built by the Athenians.

Note 6, page 158.

Constantinople is said to have resisted eighteen sieges.

Note 7, page 159.

Constantine Paleologus.

Note 8, page 161.

An ancient British prince,—who, with his whole family, sailed westward, in search of the happy islands, but never returned.

Note 9, page 161.

Plato.

Note 10, page 164.

A bishop is said to have suggested to the emperor, Charles the

Fifth, the necessity of introducing Negro slaves into his American colonies.

Note 11, page 164.

The Rabbins have a tradition, which pretends that the crimes and follies that disgrace the latter part of Solomon's history, were committed by the Prince of the Demons, in the likeness of the Jewish monarch.

Note 12, page 165.

The natives of Chili long resisted the Spaniards; and, it is said, could never be subdued.

Note 13, page 167.

Xerxes.

Note 14, page 167.

Canute.

Note 15, page 172.

Constantinople was so called by the Latins.

Note 16, page 172.

Weeds and wild flowers, cast by the waves on the western coasts of Europe, are said to have first suggested to Columbus the existence of America.

Note 17, page 172.

It is well known that many caverns, in the West Indian Isles, are almost filled with the bones of the aborigines.

Note 18, page 172.

The Hindoos say, that Timour (or Tamerlane), in the invasion of their country, broke open the tomb of one of their kings; in which he found immense treasures—apparently gold and jewels—but which, as soon as he touched them, turned to ashes.

Note 19, page 174.

The author confesses this idea to have been taken from Sir Walter Scott's ballad of 'St. John's Eve.'

Note 20, page 175.

The Chinese claim to be the inventors of gunpowder.

MISCELLANEOUS POEMS.

PART II.

MISCELLANEOUS POEMS.

THE POET'S PRAYER.

Spirit of Freedom!—is thy path
  Upon the mountains yet,—
Where oft the soaring eagle hath
  Thee, with the morning, met?—
Or have thy footsteps ever been
  Among the homes of men,
When the world wore her early green,
  Undimmed, undeluged then?—
For still a deathless dream of thee
  Lights up her fading memory!

Is it thy voice we hear, where sweep
  The rivers, in their might,—
Or forests send their murmurs deep
  Upon the winds of night?—
Thy voice, that gave the Grecian lyre
  Its glorious tones, of old,
And woke, in Erin's heart, the fire
  That never yet grew cold,—
But even from hope's ashes rose,
  The phœnix of a thousand woes!

Where shall thy few and faithful bow,—
    Whose early love remains?
For earth hath no such altar, now,
    Among her thousand fanes:
She heard the music of thy fame,
    From many an ancient shrine;
The nations called them by thy name,—
    But yet they *were* not thine;
Thou hast no temples left—but tombs:
    I call thee from *their* glorious glooms!

Oh! breathe upon my nameless lyre—
    The loved of lonely years—
And give it all my country's fire,
    Without my country's tears!
But, if the sorrow of the land
    Must mingle with its lay,
Oh! touch it with thine own bright hand,
    To wipe those tears away!
And let its latest breathings be
    A vesper hymn of hope—and thee!

THE STARS OF NIGHT.

Whence are your glorious goings forth,—
  Ye children of the sky,
In whose bright silence seems the power
  Of all eternity?
For time hath let his shadow fall
  O'er many an ancient light;
But ye walk above, in brightness still—
  O, glorious stars of night!

The vestal lamp in Grecian fane
  Hath faded long ago;—
On Persian hills the worshipped flame
  Hath lost its ancient glow;—
And long the heaven-sent fire is gone,
  With Salem's temple bright;—
But *ye* watch o'er wandering Israel, yet,
  O, changeless stars of night!

Long have ye looked upon the earth,
  O'er vale and mountain-brow;
Ye saw the ancient cities rise,
  Ye gild their ruins, now:
Ye beam upon the cottage home—
  The conqueror's path of might;
And shed your light alike on all,
  O, priceless stars of night!

And where are they, who learned from you
   The fates of coming time,—
Ere yet the pyramids arose
   Amid their desert clime?
Yet still in wilds and deserts far,
   Ye bless the watcher's sight,—
And shine where bark hath never been,
   O, lonely stars of night!

Much have ye seen of human tears—
   Of human hope and love,—
And fearful deeds of darkness, too,—
   Ye witnesses above!
Say, will that blackening record live
   For ever in your sight,
Watching for judgment on the earth,—
   O, sleepless stars of night!

How glorious was your song, that rose
   With the first morning's dawn!
And still, amid our summer sky,
   Its echo lingers on:—
Though ye have shone on many a grave,
   Since Eden's early blight,
Ye tell of hope and glory, still,—
   O, deathless stars of night!

THE MARTYR'S FAREWELL.

As night, with all her silent stars,
  Was fading fast away,
A doomed one, through his prison bars,
  Looked on the dawning day:—
For he had seen its glory break
  On many a vigil past;
And well, then, might the martyr wake—
  That morn would be his last!

He saw, afar, the eastern sky
  Bright with the coming sun,
And triumph lighted up his eye,—
  Like one whose work was done;—
Yet mingled with a strange regret
  Of deep undying love,—
He wept no treasure here—and yet
  His seemed not all above!

Grieved he for friendship's faith, that clung
  To him and could not part?
Or early hope?—for he was young
  In years—but not in heart!

Oh! not in heart—for he had seen
　　The glory pass away,
And fierce, around his path, had been
　　The tempest of the day.

Nor home nor friends were his;—for truth,
　　An early stranger grown,
It was not hard to die in youth,
　　Since he had lived alone:—
But, in that dewy hour of peace,
　　The frozen fount awoke,—
And thus, amid his loneliness,
　　The youthful sufferer spoke:—

" Thou art come, in all thy splendour, back,
　　O, bright and blessed day!
And I have marked thy golden track
　　O'er mountains far away:—
But now my changeless home is nigh,
　　My weary wandering o'er,
O, summer morn! farewell!—for I
　　Shall see thy face no more!

" How dim the gold of earth hath grown,—
　　How vain its peace or strife,—
Since to my spirit's sight was shown
　　The promised land of life!

And earthly hopes and kindred ties
   Were cast away, at will,—
But the love of you, O glorious skies!
   It lingers with me still.

" And yet, I had a dream, last night,
   Of sunny glens and green,—
Where shone my long-lost summers, bright
   As if no change had been!
And one—my early-loved—whose way
   Lies, now, through brighter bowers,—
But wherefore comes *her* memory
   Upon my dying hours!

" Hath not the Highest summoned me
   To endless life and light,
With those, upon the glassy sea,
   Who kept their garments white?—
Why gaze upon a desert-soil?
   My portion is not here;—
Long, long have been the strife and toil,—
   But now, the crown is near!

" Yet many hearts have borne, indeed,
   The cross the martyr bears,
And thought they sowed the precious seed—
   But only planted tares:—

And some have deemed that all was o'er
  When death had sealed the brow;—
Such dark thoughts never came, before,—
  Why do they cross me, now?

" God of the morning! let thy dew
  Fall on a blasted tree!
And breathe upon my country, too,
  Thy word that stilled the sea!—
Shall not some voice of power go forth—
  Some banner wave again—
For faith and freedom, on the earth?
  Though *we* have striven in vain!

" There shone the sun's first rising ray,—
  Bright as the hope of youth;
So bursts upon my soul the day
  Of everlasting truth!
For now I see eternal light
  The darkening clouds dispel,—
And go where comes no storm or night—
  Sun, moon and stars—farewell!"

WORDS.

WORDS—household words!—that linger on
  When household love is past,
And keep our childhood's tender tone
  About us, to the last;—
Like pleasant streams that murmur yet
  Of valleys far and green,
And make the pilgrim's heart forget
  The deserts spread between:
For sin and sorrow have no part
In that bright Ennoe of the heart.

Words—words of hope!—oh! long believed,
  As oracles of old,
When stars of promise have deceived,
  And beacon-fires grown cold!
Though still, upon time's stormy steeps,
  Such sounds are faint and few,
Yet oft from cold and stranger lips
  Hath fallen that blessed dew,—
That, like the rock-kept rain, remained
When many a sweeter fount was drained.

Words—words of love!—the ocean-pearl
  May slumber far and deep,
Though tempests wake or breezes curl
  The wave that hides its sleep;

So, deep in memory's hidden cells,
    The winds of life pass o'er
Those treasured words, whose music swells,
    Perchance, for us no more,—
But, Memnon-like, its echoes fill
The early-ruined temples, still.

Words—mighty words!—we see your power,
    Where'er the sun looks down
On forest-tree or fortress-tower,
    Or desert bare and brown;—
The power that, by old Tiber's wave,
    Could rouse the Roman ire,
And wake to war the Indian brave,
    Beside his council fire,—
Or call the flower of Gothic shields,
To find their rest in Syrian fields.

That mystic power is with us, still,—
    To wake the waves of strife,
Or breathe in tones of love, that thrill
    The sweetest chords of life:—
But if from mortal lips be poured
    Such spells of wondrous might,
What glorious wisdom filled *His* word
    Who spake—and there was light!
Well may that mighty Word restore
The morning of the world once more!

THE BELLS OF LIMERICK.

This poem was suggested by a tradition, given in the British
Encyclopedia.

Oh! bright on the silvery Shannon lies
  The light of the setting sun,
And stately the city's spires arise, .
  Where the isle's last field was won!
But now, no stain of the battle's blood
Remains, to sully that peaceful flood,—
Nor sound in the summer-evening swells,
Save that of St. Mary's vesper bells.

There came a late and a lonely boat,
  O'er the shining river's breast;
And it bore, from a land far, far remote,
  A sad and a stranger guest:—
A darker tint had tinged his brow
Than the skies that bent above him, now,
Could give their sons—and a brighter beam
Had shone on his youth, by Tiber's stream.

His was the peerless land of song,
  By the Muses blest, of yore;
But his steps had wandered, far and long,
  From the bright Hesperian shore:

And his early home was a darkened spot,—
For the love, that brightened his hearth, was not;
And heavy and chill the clouds of age
Fell on his lonely pilgrimage.

But still, in his memory's echo, swelled
    A sweet and a solemn chime,—
That oft, through the golden twilight pealed,
    In his own far southern clime:—
Oh! many a city and many a shore
Had the weary pilgrim wandered o'er,—
But they never sent to his aged ear
The sounds he had loved—and pined to hear!

Yet why doth the stranger start,—and turn
    From his lonely musings, now?
And why doth such glowing gladness burn
    In his aged eye and brow?
'Tis only the vesper bells, again,
That ring from St. Mary's sacred fane,—
But oh! to the wanderer's heart they tell
Of scenes and voices remembered well!

His arm was strong, and his hope was bright,
    When he tuned to melody
Those vesper bells, in the cloudless light
    Of his own Italian sky;—
And now, on a distant northern shore,
That music breathed on his heart once more—

Though the strength and hope of his years were past—
As sweet as when he heard it last!

For the light of many a twilight hour,
   And the breath of many a strain,
From cottage porch, and from myrtle bower,
   With that sound returned again:—
And the wanderer listened, like one whose soul
Had found the path to its early goal,—
But his eyes were fixed, and his very breath
Seemed hushed in the changeless hush of death!

Fainter and fainter the last low note
   On the waters died away;
And the rowers paused,—for the lonely boat
   By the stately city lay.
But the wanderer moved not—spoke not—still,
Though the dews of night fell fast and chill,
And strangers lifted his drooping head,—
But they found that the weary soul had fled!

Oh! strange were the yearning thoughts and fond
   Round that lone heart's ruined shrine,—
As the Hebrew's thirst for the fount beyond
   Philistia's leaguering line!
But the sounds, that in life he loved the best,
May peal, unheeded, above his rest,—
For still, through the summer twilight, swells
The sound of St. Mary's vesper bells!

o

THE UNSENT MESSENGER.

My song is of forgotten years,
Whose glory now is dim,—
Or only to the bard appears
In visions born for him;—
The years when Theban glory shone,
And Memphis knew no ruined throne,
Nor sorrow mingled with the tone
Of Memnon's morning hymn,—
For then his harp was newly strung,
And even the desert's heart was young!

And brightly Egypt's harvest fell
Beneath the reaper's hand,
As rose the reaper's song, to swell
The chorus of the land:—
How oft had harvest blessed the shore!—
But ne'er had been such joy before,
Where glowed the vineyard's purple store,
Or bent the gleaner band;
For famine's fearful reign was past,
And wonted plenty smiled, at last.

Forth from the Memphian palace, then,
There came a sudden sound

Of mingled grief and joy,—as when
The Nile's young bride was crowned,
And kindred sorrow deep and strong
Arose above her bridal song,
A moment heard amid the throng
And then for ever drowned—
Like her it mourned—with wilder joy
Than Saturnalian revelry!

Yet ne'er the bridal of the Nile
Such wild emotions woke,
As now, in his imperial pile,
On Pharaoh's quiet broke:
For, through the din of mingled cries,
He heard his vizier's voice arise—
The early trusted one and wise—
'Twas Joseph's heart that spoke,—
Revealing to his brethren, there,
How strong its first affections were!

Oh! mighty was the love, and strange,
That had forgiven so much,
And yet survived his fortune's change
And Time's transmuting touch;
Which, like the fairy wand of old,
Had turned to purple and to gold
His prison garb—yet ne'er unrolled
To man a page of such

Unsought and unrewarded love,
Save His—*our* Joseph, from above!

And one went forth among the sheaves,
To tell the wondrous tale,—
There, where the Nile his bounty leaves
In Delta's pleasant vale:
The reaper paused, and lent an ear—
The peasant stayed the laden steer—
And Egypt heard, like words of cheer,
The mighty vizier's wail—
Who seemed an angel, sent to save
Her famished thousands from the grave.

" Oh! could the wandering streams impart
The tidings, as they run,
How would it cheer the father's heart
To hear of his lost son!
But Israel's tents are far away"—
So spake a shepherd old and gray,—
For he was childless, and his day
Of toil was almost done;—
But on went sickle, steer and steed,—
And there was none to hear or heed,

Save one!—a maid of stately tread,
Of fair and lofty mould;
Though sprung from Egypt's ancient dread—
The shepherd-kings of old—

Yet now, she plied the peasant's toil,
And won her portion from the soil,
And bore the gleaner's bloodless spoil—
More precious far than gold.
But, ere the old man's speech was past,
That burthen at his feet was cast.

She bound the robe around her breast,
The sandals to her feet,
And journeyed onward, from the west,
As fawn in forest fleet:—
And many a vale of corn and wine,
And many a gorgeous eastern shrine,
She saw, in distant splendour, shine,—
Till evening, mildly sweet,
With saving dew and breath of balm,
Descended on the desert-palm.

And then, her glance a moment turned,
As onward still she pressed,
Where, far and bright, behind her, burned
Her own, her glorious west:
But wide the wastes of trackless sand
Around her lonely path expand,—
Till bright before her Canaan's land
Spread forth its vales of rest,—
Where lofty palm and cedar blent
Their shadows over Jacob's tent!

Old Israel sat in solitude,
Amid his weary age,
And sad and silently reviewed
His life's tear-blotted page:—
Perchance the errors of his youth—
His brother's early wrong and ruth—
Arose, in all the power of truth,
Upon the lonely sage;—
Perchance he mused on Joseph's doom,—
Or his young mother's early tomb!

Or did his absent children fill
Their father's hour of thought,
With dreams of yet more dreaded ill
Than all the past had brought?—
For he had reached the twilight time,
When shadows lengthen—and the chime
Of life's last curfew, though sublime,
With boding power is fraught,—
And knew not that before him stood
That gentle messenger of good.

But, as the thunder-cloud its shower
To the parched desert gives,
The maiden's message came, that hour—
" Arise—for Joseph lives !"
Oh! would her words so wildly brief
Repay his years of hopeless grief?

Alas! the winter's withered leaf
No summer's breath revives,—
Yet Jacob's soul rejoiced to hear,
And blessed the unsent messenger.

 " The blessing of the love that drew
Thy steps through desert ways—
The blessing of the heart made new,
Amid its winter days—
The blessing of the feet that bring
Glad tidings, like the welcome wing
Of Noah's dove—be on thy spring,
Child of an alien race!
For ne'er, in Israel's tribes, shall shine
A fame or fate more bright than thine!"

 Ah! lonely, on her homeward track,
That way-worn maiden sped;
But bore the stranger's blessing back
Upon her youthful head.
Yet still, in lowly toil she bent,
While many a harvest came and went,
And many a flowery spring was sent,
And glorious summer shed,
On Egypt's fair and fruitful plains—
Where, now, eternal ruin reigns!

 But when her youth had reached, at last,
The glory of its prime,

Ere yet upon her brow was cast
One darkening shade of time,—
When stars were fading, one by one,
As redly rose the harvest sun,
And reapers' task was just begun,—
To the far eastern clime
The maiden took her way, once more,—
But not through deserts, as of yore!

Her wreath was now a radiant crown—
Her robe the rainbow bright—
Her path where morning's star went down,
Beyond the distant height!
And shepherds, with astonished eyes,
Beheld her fearless footsteps rise,
Near—and yet nearer—to the skies,
Till, in the early light,
She paused, amid the boundless air,—
Like some bright spirit lingering there!

Then, like a barrier, backward rolled
The everlasting blue;
And portals, bright as Ophir's gold,
Received her from their view!
And they who saw that glory, gazed
No more where earthly splendours blazed,—
In vain the Pyramids were raised—
In vain the cities grew,—

For nought could win their earnest eyes
From the bright hills and blessed skies!

   And still the heavens and hills were bright;
But still they looked in vain,—
For never on their yearning sight
Such glory burst again!
Nor ever more the maid returned;
Though many a royal race was urned,—
And Egypt, in her silence, mourned
O'er fallen tower and fane;
But these were nought to her, for whom
Eternity could find no tomb!

   And had that mourner's blessing kept
Her beauty from the grave,—
While o'er the pride of nations swept
The all-devouring wave?—
Oh! then, how blessed still must be
The task of those, whose footsteps flee
To bear glad tidings, swift and free
As summer rains—that save
The dying flowers,—and, viewless, rise,
With their rich odours, to the skies!

THE EMIGRANT'S REQUEST.

———

" O friends—dear friends! if a thought remain
  Of our childhood's vanished day,
When the joy of the summer comes again,
  And my steps are far away,—
Some gentle drops from the founts that flow
  So sweet in the sultry hours,
Like an offering poured to the past, bestow
  On my lonely garden flowers!

The flowers I have left, and loved so well,—
  For their early blossoms wore
The hues that still in my memory dwell—
  But they bloom for me no more!
My home is far, in a brighter clime,
  Where the southern blooms expand,
But my heart grows sad, in the summer time,
  For the flowers of its native land!

The holy haunts of my childhood's love,
  And its joy, were still with them,—
When my dearest wealth was the forest dove,
  Or the violet's purple gem.

How fast the heart's young myrtles grew!—
    Yet their bloom was brightly fleet;
For it changed to the cypress' sombre hue—
    But the flowers were ever sweet!

O, friends! you may watch the wild-bird's wing,
    When it seeks the ocean-track,—
But await the breath of the coming spring—
    It will waft the wanderer back;—
But where is the spring-time that can give
    My voice to your distant bowers?—
Oh! then let my lingering memory live
    In the breath of those home-born flowers!"

YOUTH AND AGE.

It was where shone the setting sun,
  Upon the vineyards bright,—
A vintage band, their labours done,
  Were gathered in its light:—
And none were sad or silent, then,
  Amid that joyous throng,
For vale and grove gave back again
  The sound of dance and song.

There came a man, of silver hair,
  Upon his lonely way;
But wherefore paused the pilgrim, there,
  Among the young and gay?—
He paused, till rose the latest tears
  Which yet remained unshed,
As, in the twilight of his years,
  The lonely wanderer said:—

" I ask not now for friendship's eyes,
  Nor tones the grave hath stilled,—
For all life's early prophecies—
  The bright, but unfulfilled!—
For meteors of the heart, that wane
  Before the torch of truth,—
O, Time! I ask not these again—
  But give me back my youth!"

Then rose a dark-eyed maiden's song
  From out that festal band,—
The brightest daughter of the throng,
  The star of all her land!
No eye had seen the shade of woe
  Her morning splendours dim;—
Yet thus, with roses on her brow,
  That maiden answered him:—

"O, man of many summers! say,
  Why turns thy spirit back,
When, now, the evening's latest ray
  Is on its homeward track?
Thy trial-day is near its close,
  Thy pilgrim-journey o'er,—
Then rather keep thy tears for those
  The desert lies before!

"For they must wander from the wells
  That cheered their early ways,
To wastes wherein no fountain swells—
  The unredeemed of days!
Must weep for many a withered gourd,
  Whose shade they loved the best,—
For many a sweet but broken chord,
  Before they reach their rest.

"Why mournest thou thy perished spring?—
  It came but to depart;—

Oh! early come the storms, that bring
  The winter of the heart!
Old age, indeed, around his brow
  Hath autumn's dimness hung;
But there are darker clouds, that throw
  Their shadows on the young!

" For some have felt the winter's tears
  Upon the summer's prime,
And seen the glory of their years
  Grow dim before the time;—
Or sunk for ever, while they wore
  Life's yet unsullied crown,—
Like laden barks, with all their store,
  To ocean-depths gone down!"

She ceased:—the wanderer went his way;—
  The vintage came, again;
And he returned, when dying day
  Was bright on sky and plain:
He saw the dancers, as of yore—
  He saw the vineyards bloom,—
But the dark-eyed maid he saw no more,—
  For SHE had found the tomb!

LA PEROUSE.

His country's banner to the gale
  The sea-bound warrior gave,
And gathered to his spreading sail
  The noble, wise and brave:
And hope went with the young and gay,
  Who left their sunny shore
For isles of promise far away,—
  But ne'er were heard of more![1]

Yet far their ocean chief had been,
  In sunlight, storm and gloom,—
On every shore his flag was seen—
  But who hath seen his tomb!
The stars of night and dews of morn
  Earth's seasons still restore,—
But the land looked long for their return—
  They ne'er were heard of more!

Oh! had they found, mid trackless sea,
  Some glorious land, enshrined,
Where lived no lingering memory
  Of all they left behind?—

For many a brave bark sought, in vain,
   Their wandering to explore,—
But day or night, on land or main,
   They ne'er were heard of more!

Time passed away—on darkest hair
   It brought the snow of years,—
Till faith had ceased her fruitless prayer,
   And love forgot her tears:
And wasted heart and weary hand
   The grave alike closed o'er,—
Dark things were known of every land—
   They ne'er were heard of more!

Alas! their land, beyond the waves,
   Hath felt both sword and flame,—
And given her brave to stranger-graves,
   Who left her deathless fame!—
But still, though tried and tempest-tost
   As none have been before,
She keeps the memory of the lost,—
   Who ne'er were heard of more!

THE SKY.

The sky—how its far depths shine,
   In the pomp of summer days,—
Lit up, like an everlasting shrine,
   For the nations' upward gaze!
The nations perish—but it remains,
   In its glory ever new,—
For the cloud and the tempest leave no stains
   On its robe of peerless blue.

We have sought the shrines of old,—
   They were built by mighty hands;
Yet they lie on the Thracian mountains cold,
   And they strew the Theban sands:—
But ever the starry legions march
   In their glorious paths on high,—
For a mightier builder raised the arch
   Of the still imperial sky!

We have wandered, far and wide,
   From the path of our better years,—
We have turned from pleasant springs aside,
   To the streams of strife and tears:—
We have laid our love on the shrines of clay,—
   We have toiled for wealth and fame,—
And the love and the glory passed away,—
   But we found *it* still the same.

Still bending o'er the hills,
　　As our childhood saw it bend,—
And smiling on earth, through all her ills,
　　Like a fair and faithful friend:
For it smiles on us when the world grows strange,
　　And our summers have gone by!—
Oh! hopes may wither and hearts may change,
　　But thou fadest not, bright sky!

The silent sage looks up to thee,
　　In his musings calm and deep;
And the mariner, on the star-lit sea,
　　When the winds and waters sleep;
The savage looks on thy lighted face,
　　Through the dark and shadowy pines,—
For he sees his God in the lonely place
　　Where thy changeful glory shines!

Thou speak'st to every ear,
　　With a voice for every heart,—
In the thunder's solemn tones of fear,
　　Or the soft wind's sighing art:—
And we look away, from the withering flowers
　　And graves that round us lie,
Where our hopes are urned,—to the starry bowers
　　Of the bright and boundless sky!

ROUSTAN.

The desert heard his early fame;
  Among her brightest spears
His sword was known,—and far his name,
  Though few and green his years.
But when the dates were falling fast,
  And fiery winds at rest,
That young and fearless warrior passed
  The waters of the west.

Say, was it love of Christian maid,
  That lured his steps so far,—
Or dream of brighter regions, spread
  Beneath the western star?
Ah! more he loved the desert land
  Of tribes that know no thrall;—
But, at a stranger chief's command,
  The Arab left them all!

He left the ever-cloudless day—
  The glorious palms and green,—
With founts that in their shadow lay,
  Where happy hours had been:

But homes grew sad, by tree and stream,
  Upon that desert shore,—
For their best and bravest followed him,—
  But they returned no more!

O'er many a far and frozen coast,
  Through many a northern land,
A chief among the Gallic host,
  The Arab led his band;—
Where wide the storm of battle hailed,
  And wider yawned its grave,
And even the Gallic spirit quailed,—
  The Arab still was brave.

Till—as the sandy billows fall,
  When sinks the desert blast—
They fell around him, one and all,—
  And he was left the last:
Yet still, in many a field renowned,
  He bore a leader's part,—
And shared the blood-bought wreath that crowned
  The sovereign of his heart.

And when the flood of fortune changed,
  And friends were false or few,—
When hope was faint, and love estranged,
  The Arab still was true!

But ne'er his after joy or grief
   May lyre or pen relate,—
For the clouds that closed around his chief,
   Have veiled the Arab's fate!

But glory to the fearless faith
   That fortune could not shake!—
And blessings on the love that death
   Might seal, but never break!
His spirit's early-worshipped sun
   Hath sunk in shadows dim,—
But the world itself had never won
   The love that went with him!

COPAN.

'Twas in the western wilderness
    Of everlasting trees,—
Where rose no voice and waved no tress
    Upon the lonely breeze,—
Where never light of sun or star
    Might shine through bower or glade;—
Why came the stranger, then, so far,
    To pierce its depth of shade?

Did not his childhood's eye the land
    Of ancient woods behold,
In summer's greenness darkly grand,
    Or autumn's gorgeous gold?
Had he not heard the tempest sweep
    Through forests vast and hoar,
Like some yet undiscovered deep
    Lone sounding on its shore?

Yes!—but from southern wilds there came
    A voice of olden time,—
An echo of departed fame
    Dwelt in that golden clime:

And there, the dauntless traveller found[2]
  His toil repaid at last,—
Where wreaths of countless summers crowned
  A city of the past!

The birds had sung its solitude,
  While silent ages swept,—
And palm-trees, where its altars stood,
  Their voiceless vigil kept:
And flowers grew fair, amid the homes
  Of a departed race,—
Whose skill had raised the ruined domes
  Of that green desert place.

Was this, when Greece and time were young,
  The land of Plato's dreams,—
Whose glory round his visions hung,
  By far and classic streams?
Or had its fading splendour shone
  Like sunset o'er the seas,
And lit, through trackless waves, alone,
  The fearless Genoese?

How have they perished from the earth!—
  By lyre and pen forgot,
Alike their destiny and birth,
  They were—and they are not!

Time swept into oblivion's womb
　Their glory and their power,—
And ancient forests spread their gloom
　O'er temple, tomb and tower.

For nature's hand is mighty, still;
　The thrones of earth decay,—
The sword of war, the pen of skill
　And wisdom, pass away,—
But wide she spreads her leafy pall,
　Or bids the harvest wave,—
And the glory, and the conquest, all
　Are thine, devouring grave!

THE CHILD AND THE ROSE.

The summer shines forth, in her splendour and pride,—
Though she sees but a hut on the lone mountain-side;
Yet mark, where a rose-tree hath bloomed in the wild,
How gazes upon it the cottager's child!
Ah! long in that rose have been centered the care
And hope of the young heart who planted it there;
And now the bright beams of the morning are shed
Where its first-opened blossom hangs, dewy and red.

But see, where, in silence, the peasant-boy stands,
With his bright-flashing eye and his wonder-clasped
hands!
He fears not the future, he weeps not the past,
Though it may be *that* joy is his first, and his last.
Gaze on, thou young dreamer!—of gladness, that now
Illumines thy spirit and brightens thy brow,
Through all its far changes, life ne'er shall give back
The early-lost sunshine, to lighten thy track.

Oh! brilliant the noon of thy fortunes may be,—
For the future is fruitful in promise for thee;
There's a grace in thy steps, there's a light in thine eyes,
That tell of a spirit from darkness to rise:—

The moonlight of love may be shed on thy youth,
And thine age may rejoice in some changeless heart's
      truth,—
And thy day, which in cloud and in shadow arose,
In the brightness of glory's own sunset may close.

But oft, 'mid the sweetness thy youth scatters down,—
And oft through the light of thy coming renown,—
Shall thy spirit return to the joy it has known
With the rose-tree that bloomed on the mountains, alone.
Ah! never again can the summers restore
The bloom of the heart, when its freshness is o'er;
They may light thee to glory, to pleasure, to power—
But can never restore thee thy joy of this hour!

THE FRENCH ARMY AT CARNAK.

It was where Carnak's temples stood,
 Amid the morn, alone,—
But from their depth of solitude
 Even Memnon's voice was gone;
For time had hushed his lyre, at last,
 Though still, in marble pride,
Far was his lonely shadow cast
 Upon the desert wide.

There rose a sound on that still air,
 Like rushing streams afar,
As with its conquering eagles, there
 Came on the Gallic war!
It came where Time had power, no more,
 To waste, on Theban walls,
But hung the hush of ages o'er
 Those long-forsaken halls!

Like voices that had long been lost,
 The ancient echoes woke,—
As, all at once, that stranger host
 Their joy and wonder spoke:—
There were the young, the brave, the wise,—
 A nation's gathered might;
And well might every heart rejoice
 To see that glorious sight!

In one brief moment, all forgot
    Their onward path of war,—
Nay, in that hour, remembered not
    The land of vines, afar:—
Long from that city's grave a gleam
    Had o'er the nations shone:—
How would she haunt each future dream,
    For ever vast and lone!

And what were *thy* deep thoughts, that hour,
    Chief of those warrior men?
Were they of ancient thrones and power,
    Or of the desert, then?—
Or did old Thebes—in all the world
    The mightiest desolate—
Show, in her pall of silence furled,
    Thy far and future fate?

None—none can tell!—the morning's light
    A wondrous splendour shed,
Around that host of banners bright,
    And city of the dead;
They left her, by the lonely stream,
    Where burns the Afric day;
And still, the sleeping desert's dream,
    She stands,—but where are they!

"I HAVE MISSED MY DESTINY."

These are said to have been the words of Buonaparte, when obliged to raise the siege of Acre.

Ah! why were such words in thy weariness spoken,
  Thou sleeper, whose memory fades not away?
Were they flung from thy heart, like an early-sent token
  Of clouds that should darken the close of thy day?
And oh! was it thus, when the flood of thy glory
  The walls of old Acre alone might resist,
Thou saw'st thine own niche in the temple of story,
    Still bright—with the promise thy fortunes have
      missed?

We know not:—but who, that hath looked on the pages
  Of wisdom which brighten the volume of time,—
And traced, through the far-fading twilight of ages,
  The feeble who sink or the mighty who climb—
Hath heard not thy words, in the power of their sadness,
  Arise from the depths of the heart or the grave,—
Re-echoed from fields trampled down by the madness
  Of battle, or borne from the wrecks of the wave?
For weary and wide were the wastes *they* have wandered,
  Whose names have been highest in glory's proud list,—

And bright were the treasures of hope that they squan-
dered
  Who perished—and saw but their destiny missed!

They sought for the stream—when the fountain was
near them,
  They pined for the shade when the forest was green;
And sunshine, that rose on the desert to cheer them,
  But brightened the cloud that came darkly between.
Alas! for the brightness that beckons to danger,
  Where love cannot lighten or friendship assist,—
For they went, as they came, with the heart of the
stranger,
  And left us to gather the gems they had missed.

The prodigal knows not the wealth he has wasted,
  Till only the husks and his hunger remain;
The mariner mourns not the fountain untasted
  Till nothing is left but the brine of the main:—
And thus it is, still, with the world's brightest dreamers
  Who rise in its tumults, or fall in its strife,
Too late comes the light that reveals the false-seemers,
  Too late, in its wisdom, the lesson of life!
But green grows the grave, in its silence, before them—
  It leads to the land where no deserts exist;
And only eternity's spring can restore them
  The glory and hope of their destiny missed!

THE CYPRESS OF SOMME.

Thou art not sad, green cypress tree![2]
　Though bards have given to woe
Thy shadow spread so darkly free;—
　Hast thou no graves, below?
No sigh thy summer foliage fills,
　Save twilight's dying breath,—
Amid the glory of the hills
　Is there no place for death?

Yet wherefore should thy shadow fling
　Its greenness on the grave,
When thou hast shared the earliest spring
　Of Him who came to save!
Perchance, thy bursting branches heard,
　From wandering breeze or star,
Some tone of angel gladness, stirred
　In Bethlehem's vale, afar!

And still, when first the morning wakes,
　And stars begin to set,
Some echo of that music breaks
　Thy dewy silence yet:—

What all the world hath lost so long,
  Remains it still with thee,—
The memory of that blessed song?
  Thou lonely cypress tree!

Was it that glorious memory, say!
  That kept thine age so green,—
When thousand forests passed away,
  As if they ne'er had been?
The laurel of Apollo's love
  From Delphian heights is gone,—
And the glory of the cedar grove
  Is fallen, on Lebanon;—

But harmless, o'er thy sombre shade,
  The centuries have rolled,
Thy life has seen the nations fade,
  And Rome herself grow old:
And still untouched by time or tears,
  Thy boughs are waving free,
In the greenness of two thousand years,—
  Thou lonely cypress tree!

Long—long, he sleeps, the fearless lord
  Of Gallic lance and shield,
Who turned on thee his shattered sword,
  From Pavia's fatal field!

His knightly fame is in the dust,—
   With all its gorgeous glare,—
But thou bearest, as a sacred trust,
   The badge of his despair!

And there was one, who wreaked his wrath
   On holy things and hoar,—
Yet turned, to spare thee, from his path,
   Who never turned before:—
The haughty heart hath bowed to death,
   That reverenced only thee;
But *thou* strengthenest, still, the peasant's faith,—
   O, lonely cypress tree!

THE HOPE OF THE RESURRECTION.

Suggested by the remarks of an African Chief, which are given in
the Bechuana Mission.

Thy voice hath filled our forest shades,
 Child of the sunless shore!
For never heard the ancient glades
 Such wondrous words before.
Though bards our land of palms have filled
 With tales of joy or dread,—
Yet thou, alone, our souls hast thrilled
 With tidings of her dead.

The men of old, who slept in death,
 Before the forests grew,
Whose glory faded here beneath,
 While yet the hills were new,—
The warriors famed in battles o'er,
 Of whom our fathers spake,—
The wise, whose wisdom shines no more,—
 Stranger, will they awake?

The foes who fell in thousand fights,
 Beneath my conquering brand,—
Whose bones have strewn the Caffir's heights,
 The Bushman's lonely land,—
The young, who shared my warrior-way,
 But found an early urn,—

And the roses of my youth's bright day—
  Stranger, will they return?

My mother's face was fair to see—
  My father's glance was bright,—
But long ago the grave from me
  Hath hid their blessed light;
Still sweeter was the sunshine shed
  By my lost children's eyes,
That beam upon me from the dead,—
  Stranger, will they arise?

Was it some green grave's early guest,
  Who loved thee long and well,
That left the land of dreamless rest,
  Such blessed truths to tell?
For we have had our wise ones, too,
  Who feared not death's abyss,—
The strong in hope, in love the true,—
  But none that dreamed of this!

Yet if the grave restore to life
  Her ransomed spoils again,
And ever hide the hate and strife
  That died with wayward men;—
How hath my spirit missed the star
  That guides our steps above;
Since only earth was given to war,—
  That better land to love!

THE PRAYER OF CHILDHOOD.

She was a child of sunny hair,
 And bright but thoughtful brow,—
And face that seemed so wondrous fair,
 It haunts my visions, now,—
As I heard her pour her evening prayer,
 Beneath the olive bough!

And ah! the prayer the orphan said,
 Was sadly fond and free,—
For a young mother early dead,
 And a father far at sea;—
Yet when she blessed each kindred head,
 I heard her pray for me!

For me!—oh! many a storm hath burst,
 And many a cloud hath loured
Upon my lonely path, since first
 That gentle prayer was poured:—
But it was with me, in the worst,
 Like an unfading gourd!

And never from my spirit passed
    The dew so strangely shed,—
Though time and sorrow both have cast
    Their ashes on my head;—
Till I deemed that haunting prayer, at last,
    The blessing of the dead.

No more was to mine eyes revealed
    That gentle orphan's face,—
Years and their chances have concealed
    Her after dwelling-place;—
And it may be, that the grave hath sealed
    Those lips of love and grace:—

But childhood's lessons from my heart
    Have past like sounds of air,—
And voices, tuned by love's own art,
    Have left no echoes there,—
Yet it ne'er forgot its blessed part
    In that young orphan's prayer!

THE TREASURES OF THE EARTH.

What are thy treasures, Earth?—what stores
  Lie in thy darkness deep?
There, work the hidden waters—there,
  The fires that never sleep:
And depths where daylight never shone
  Upon the diamond's birth,
And gold unwept, unworshipped still,
  Are thine, thou silent Earth!

Low lie the ancient cities, long
  Forgotten of the light,—
Thou hast buried deep their multitudes,
  Their gathered wealth and might:—
And heaped up spoil, from all the past,
  Of wilderness or hearth,
Of festive hall or holy fane,—
  These are thy treasures, Earth!

Thine are the forests, of green strength
  And trackless shadow free,—
The harvest joy, the stores of life,
  For ever gush from thee;—

And fountains far, that send their streams
  In might and music forth,—
And flowers that bloom, and breathe of heaven,—
  These are thy treasures, Earth!

And more—far more!—to thee are gone
  How many a vanished race!
The famed of nations, in thy dust
  Have found a dwelling-place:—
To thee was brave blood freely poured,
  And hearts of priceless worth
Have gone, with all their glory down—
  These are *our* treasures, Earth!

And more—yet more! fond love is thine—
  Deep love around the dead;—
And o'er man's sin and sorrow, too,
  Thy garment green is spread:—
Thou hast homes for all the desolate,
  Where comes no blight or dearth;
And an unchanging welcome, still,
  For thy worn children, Earth!

THE UNKNOWN COMET.

The first faint gleam of rosy light
   Had tinged the eastern steep,—
While yet the hush of summer's night
   Hung o'er the city's sleep:
But 'mid the silence, there was one
   Who, wakeful, watched the light
Where faint the setting comet shone
   Amid the dying night.

His care had marked that stranger star,
   Since first, to mortal eyes,
Its distant glory dawned, afar
   Amid the trackless skies.
And now, it faded from his sight—
   But science sought in vain
The moment that should shed its light
   Upon our earth again.

"And hast thou walked the heavens, alone,
   Since night and day were young?
Nor paused when round thy burning zone
   The later planets sprung?
Still onward, in thy shining way,
   The glorious and the free,—

O, bright untiring herald! say,
  What may thy mission be?

" Art thou the star that woke, of old,[4]
  The home of hidden waves,
Till wide and deep the deluge rolled
  O'er nameless nations' graves?
Or was the sage Chaldean taught,
  At first, his starry lore, ·
When Babylon thy brightness caught
  Upon her towers, of yore?

" Was thine the mystic story, graved[5]
  On Egypt's marbles old?
Or flaming sword that nightly waved
  O'er Salem's sacred hold?
Or thine the boding beam that hailed[6]
  The crescent's last advance,—
When all the might of Europe failed,
  Save Sobieski's lance?

" Is it some bright unresting soul,—
  Whose loved had left our sphere,
And early gained the glorious goal,
  While yet it wandered here—
That guides thy chariot-path, on high,
  Beyond the starry bound?—
Ah,—searcher of eternity!
  When will thy lost be found?

" Full many a star, of ancient birth,
    Hath perished from its place,—
And many a glory from the earth
    Hath past, and left no trace,—
Since first thy burning wheels were driven
    Along the azure arch;
And still thy fiery course, in heaven,
    Is like a conqueror's march!

" The sacred fanes, the victor swords,
    On which thy splendour shines,—
As once it shone on Scythia's hordes
    And Hellas' matchless shrines,—
The pride of gallies on the sea,
    Of cities on the plain,—
Where—where will all these glories be,
    When thine returns, again,—

" O, meteor-guest!"—While yet he spoke,
    It faded from his view,
And morn upon the mountains broke,
    With all her light and dew!
And time, in its untiring flight,
    Made many a bright eye dim,—
But never, with returning light,
    That comet shone on him!

THE AUSTRALIAN EMIGRANT.

A bark went forth, with the morning's smile,
That bore the maids of the western isle
Far, where the southern summers shine
On the glorious world beyond the line.
Theirs was a weary lot of toil,
And their hopes were turned to a better soil,
While their tears were shed for the island-shore—
They should look on its greenness never more!

But one was there—who shed no tears!—
A girl, in the blossom of her years;—
Yet bloom had she none from the roses caught,
For her cheek was withered with early thought,—
And her young brow bore the written doom
Of a lonely heart and a distant tomb;—
But still, in the light of her starry eye,
There shone a glory that could not die!

Silent she gazed on the shore and sea,—
And ever her glance was bright and free,
Like a spirit's, bound by no kindred ties,—
(For she had none beneath the skies!)
Till the mountains faded in misty blue,—
And louder the grief around her grew:

Then, turned the maid to that mourning throng,—
And poured the power of her soul in song!

How sadly mixed was that parting strain,
That told of the talent given in vain,
And the wisdom born of deep despair:—
With the tone of triumph blending there,
Through faintest fall and through wildest swell
Was heard the voice of the heart's farewell,—
As if the dream on her memory hung
Of a wasted love!—and thus she sung:—

"Whence flow these floods of sorrow?—
    O, my gentle sisters, tell!—
Do the heart's deep fountains send their streams
    To bid the land farewell?
Like a shadow passing from us
    Is each mighty mountain's brow,—
But earth—the wide green earth—is ours,—
    We have no country now!
But, oh! the old home track,
    Where our first affections rest!
Alas! no time shall give them back—
    Our earliest and our best!

"Oh! MAN may grieve to sever
    From the hearth or from the soil,—
For still some hope, some right, was his,
    Which lived through want and toil;—

The dwellers of the forest,
    THEY may mourn their leafy lair;—
But why should WOMAN weep her land?
    She has no portion there.
Woe—woe for deeds of worth,
    That were only paid with ill!—
For to *her* the homes of earth
    Are the house of bondage, still!

" The ocean spreads around us,
    In its glory far and free,—
The hope of many a heart lies low
    Beneath that slumbering sea!
For us its depths may waken,
    In the war of wind and wave,
And the hearts, that have no portion here,
    May find it in the grave!
Yet woe for all the vanished hues
    To life's young visions given,—
And the freshness of the heart's first dews—
    It only lasts in heaven!

" We go to summers brighter
    Than o'er our childhood shone,—
But when shall we forget the isle
    Whose sorrow was our own?
It may be, love will linger long,
    Upon some broken stay

Of early hopes and early graves—
The green, the far away!—
A vision of the far-off shore
Long round our hearts shall dwell,—
But we return no more—no more!—
Ye glorious hills, farewell!"

She ceased:—for the shore was fading fast,—
She looked on it longest, then, and last:—
And the dying tones of her parting song
Remained in the hearts of the listeners, long.
—When tidings came, from the wandering band,
Of brightening days in that distant land,
Of the minstrel's fortune none could say—
She had passed, in her loneliness, away!

THE REMOVAL OF THE CHEROKEES.

The summer day's departing light
  On corn and vineyard shone,—
Where red men, driven by ruthless might,
  Had left their dwellings lone.
But 'mid their memories sweet, a maid,
  In sorrow lingered long;—
And thus, beneath her roof-tree's shade,
  Arose her parting song:—

" Farewell, our pleasant land, redeemed
  From wilderness and wild!
Where bright the stars of winter beamed,
  And summer on us smiled.
The graves grew green, in that still spot,
  Around our holy place;
But the blessing of its peace is not
  For us, the forest race!

" Alas! the stranger's arm is strong
  Upon our western shore;
The hills forget our battle song,—
  The streams are ours no more!
The falling forests utter forth
  A murmur deep and low,
That calls my people from the earth,—
  Ye glorious woods, we go!

"But go not as of old we went,—
  With woodland spear and bow;—
The arrows of the tribes are spent,
  The hunter's strength is low:
Yet nobler nations, from the land,
  Before our fathers, passed—
Where now, with iron heart and hand,
  The pale ones come at last!

" Woe—woe, for all the evil years
  Of strife, which we have seen!—
For the red woman's toil and tears!
  Brave have our warriors been,—
Yet many were the dark days given
  To them, the true of heart;
And now, the promised light from heaven
  Hath shone—but we depart!

" The hunter's path the bright sun sees—
  Then wherefore should we stay,
When the green glory of our trees
  Hath past from earth away?
No!—let us seek the land of peace,
  Where all our lost ones dwell!
We go to the far wilderness—
  Sweet home—green graves—farewell!"

THE TRUEST VOICE.

Voice of the morning!—sweetly wild
As the tameless tones of a forest child;
Breaking from rocks on the mountain steep—
Waking the wilds of the woodlands deep—
Calling the sun to his upward way,
And man to the hopes of another day!

Voice of the twilight!—sad and low,
Sighing where valley-fountains flow,—
Breathing deep by the ruined towers—
Lingering late with the folding flowers—
Stilling the throb of the ocean's breast,
And hushing the weary world to rest!

Voice of the midnight!—deeply lone,
Filling the soul with thy solemn tone,—
Calling up thoughts like the troubled waves—
Waking the echoes of ancient graves—
Telling of hidden things that lie
Far in the past eternity!

Voices of earth!—ye have many tones,
Where forests wave or the ocean moans:
There is no silence,—for deeply and strong
Rolls on the tide of eternal song,

Through nature's realms, but its holiest part
Is heard in the depths of the human heart!

Voice of the absent!—ringing still
Through the spirit's shade, like a hidden rill;—
Perchance but a lonely stream of tears,
Yet sweet with the breath of our brighter years,—
For ever thy wandering wave flows on,
Through the withered roses of summers gone!

Voice of the dead!—that return'st, at times,
Like a bird from the far untravelled climes,—
Though sent in the wintry hours of life,
And heard in the pause of the tempest's strife,
Yet breathing still of those brighter skies
That shine where our land of promise lies!

Thou speak'st in the love of long ago,
To hearts who have laid their treasures low:
Oh! the whispers of living love may change,
And its pleasant voices grow coldly strange;
But the grave is true to our early trust—
For the golden harp-string cannot rust!

THE STATUE.

Suggested by an incident, said to have occurred at one of the
festivities consequent on the Coronation of her present Majesty.

Why is thy look so strangely sad,
    Thou of the joyous clime!
While eyes are bright and hearts are glad,
    Amid the banquet's prime?
Around thee float the song and dance,
    With all their witching powers,—
Not so, methinks, thy country's glance
    Is wont to meet such hours!

Is it that time upon thy locks
    Hath early shed his snow?
Or dream'st thou of the battle shocks
    That laid thy fortunes low?
Or hath some form, amid the throng,
    Recalled the perished flame
Of early love, remembered long
    Through all thy fields of fame?

Ah, no!—thou gazest, where the light
    Of torch and taper falls
On marble, gleaming coldly bright
    Among our festive halls:
When first its cold, pale beauty fell
    Upon thy distant view,

What memories started, at its spell—
  The dark—the strangely true!

It waved up many a vanished scene
  Of battles lost and won,—
The friends whose path with thine have been—
  The deeds thy sword hath done:
What tongue or pen hath never told,
  Passed by, with soundless tread,—
Well may the revel's joy grow cold—
  Thy thoughts are with the dead!

Dream on—dream on! the silent past
  Gives up its mighty shades!
The laurels of the tomb may last,
  When even its myrtle fades.
There stands the Chief, before whose glance
  Old Europe learned to bow;
He ruled thy changeful fortunes once—
  He rules thy spirit now!

No shadow on that brow is thrown—
  No touch of time or care—
Whate'er the living may have known
  Of darkness or despair:
But glorious, still, as when in youth
  He led his conquering land,
And the marble grew to life and truth,
  Beneath Canova's hand!

Oh, blessed art!—that can reclaim
   The glorious things of clay
From death's dominion,—friend of fame,
   And conqueror of decay!
The blight that kills the mortal part
   This form shall never sere,—
And clouds, that darken hope and heart,
   Can cast no shadow here.

But thou!—for thee, such visions wake
   The thoughts that cannot sleep,
But ever on thy quiet break,
   In echoes sad and deep.
Even now, as parts the festive throng,
   I mark thee gazing back,—
Like thy land's memory, turning long
   To her lost meteor's track!

THE FOUNT OF SONG.

Where flows the fount whose living streams
   Are heard in every clime,—
Whose voice hath mingled with the dreams
   Of far departed time?
Is it where Grecian fanes lie hid
   Among the olives dim,
Or the Nile beside the pyramid
   Sends up its ceaseless hymn?

Alas! by old Castalia's wave
   The Muses meet no more;
Nor breaks from Delphi's mystic cave
   The prophet voice of yore:
Old Egypt's river hath forgot
   The Theban glory gone,
And the land of Homer knows him not—
   Yet still that fount flows on!

The sacred fount of song—whose source
   Is in the poet's soul;
Though living laurels crown its course,
   All glorious to the goal,

Yet who can tell what desert part
  Its earliest springing nursed?—
As, from the glacier's icy heart
  The mightiest rivers burst!

Perchance the wind that woke the lyre
  Was but a blighting blast,
That seared with more than tempest's ire
  The verdure where it passed:—
Perchance the fire, that seemed divine,
  On ruined altars shone,—
Or glowed like that Athenian shrine
  For deity unknown!

It is not fame, with all her spells,
  Could wake the spirit's springs,
Or call the music forth that dwells
  Amid its hidden strings:—
For evermore, through sun and cloud,
  To the first fountain true,
It flows,—but oh! ye soulless crowd,
  It never sprang for you!

The wild bird sings in forests far,
  Where foot may never be,—
The eagle meets the morning star,
  Where none his path may see;

So many a gifted heart hath kept
  Its treasures unrevealed,—
A spring whose depth in silence slept,
  A fount for ever sealed!

Woe, for the silent oracles,—
  That went, with all their lore!
For the world's early-wasted wells,
  Whose waters flow no more!
Yet one remains—no winter's wrath
  Can bind or summer dry,—
For, like our own, its onward path
  Is to eternity!

THE UNWORN CROWN.

It is well known that the messenger, who brought the intelligence
that the laureate-crown had been decreed to Tasso, found him
dying in a convent.

Cold on Torquato's silence fell
    The shadow of the tomb,—
When sounds of triumph reached his cell,
    Amid the cloister's gloom:
" Awake! the crown awaits thee now—
Come, bind the laurel to thy brow !

" Haste, where the peerless Capitol
    Two thousand years hath shone;
Arise!—for Rome and glory call
    Thee to their ancient throne;
And these had but one name of old—
Be thine with Petrarch's fame inrolled!"

" Vain voice! thou comest"—said the bard,
    " When hope itself is o'er;
But now my spirit's peace is marred
    By dreams of earth no more:—
For who would deem the mirage true,
With living waters in his view !

" Yet, I *have* loved the praise of men,
   As few will e'er avow;
How prized had been thy tidings, then!
   How worthless are they now!
Sore was the travail,—and the gain
Is found, indeed, but found in vain!

" Why came it not, when o'er my life
   A cloud of darkness hung,—
When years were lost in fruitless strife,
   But still my *heart* was young?
How hath the shower forgot the spring,
And fallen on autumn's withering!

" Long, in mine eyes, the golden sand
   Of life shone far and fair,—
Like him who saw the promised land,
   But might not enter there:
The dimness of my soul hath past,—
I see a *better* land at last!

" A land where blight hath never been—
   Where laurels never fade,
But keep the heart, too, ever green
   In their immortal shade,—
Unlike the proudest palms of earth,
That shadow but the desert's dearth.

" Yet still it lives,—my first—last—thought,
    Unchanged by time or fate:
Woe, for the blight so early caught—
    The dew that fell so late!
Woe, for the hope whose joy departs!—
For the lost love of many hearts!

" But lo, a hope of better birth!
    Eternity is given!
And all that love hath lost on earth,
    May yet be found in heaven!
Go! fling those dying laurels down—
For Tasso wins a brighter crown!"

THE DYING STRANGER.

He was a man of war and fame
   Among the sons of earth,
And long the echo of his name
   Shall live by throne and hearth:—
But his last days were dark—for fate
Had made him early desolate.

He was alone; and stranger skies
   Bent o'er him, cold and dim;—
But sun might set and star arise,
   Oh, never more for him!
For now, the shadow of the grave
Shut out the world—like Lethe's wave!

But music came, at sunset hour,—
   A faint and distant strain
Of his own land;—it had the power
   To wake his heart again,
As if the green hills called him back
Once more across the ocean track.

Was it some old victorious lay,
    Amid his laurels heard—
Or music of the battle day—
    That memory's fountain stirred?
Ah, no!—it told of dwellings low,
Among the vineyards—long ago!

For many a strangely chequered year,
    And many a changeful scene,
Had passed, since in his childhood's ear
    Those pleasant sounds had been;
And even glory's self was nought,
In the sweet memories which they brought.

They brought the summers of his youth—
    Its friends, the fair and gay—
The tender love—the blessed truth—
    The peace—that passed away;—
They brought his eyes the only tears
That dimmed their restless light for years!

Alas! was this the price of fame!
    The prize is dearly won,—
As he had found—to whom it came,
    His portion 'neath the sun:—
The sunset on his mountains lay,
While he was dying—far away!

But time and space rolled back!—that strain
  Had brought him near his home,—
There spake his early lost again,
  And bade their wanderer come;
And far his country's voice was sent—
It seemed to bless him ere he went!

Oh! calmly, on the western sky
  The wanderer gazed his last,—
As with that home-born melody
  His lonely spirit passed!
And blessed be the lyre whose breath
Was mighty, at the gates of death!

THE BARD'S FAREWELL.

'Twas where the harvest moon looked bright, and tender,
  Upon a silent forest vast and old,
Whose trees stood in the yet unshaken splendour
  Of summer's foliage, turned to glowing gold
By autumn's touch,—that withered, while it made
More rich, the leafy glory of the shade—
Like genius early wasting youth away,
  Yet shedding beauty o'er its bright decay!

There stood, amid that forest green and hoary,
  A yet more ancient ruin; which had been
A holy place, in days of Grecian story,—
  But now, its walls were wreathed with ivy green,
And through its arches the low winds sighed on,—
For god and priest and worshipper were gone,
Ages ago; yet still the temple stood,
Sacred in its untrodden solitude.

But now, a sweetly-solemn voice was blending
  With the low murmurs of the forest's might,—
As from that shrine a homeless bard was sending
  His latest song upon the wings of night.

Death's shadows were around him; and his heart
Had nothing left from which it grieved to part,—
Save the sweet lyre that thus, with tuneful swell,
Rang out the measure of his fond farewell:—

" Farewell!—for earth hath nought beside
    To love or value now;
The myrtles in my heart have died—
    The laurels on my brow:
And clouds o'er many a star have passed
    That well might song inspire,—
But thou art with me, to the last,—
    Farewell, my faithful lyre!

" All other voices have deceived—
    All other love was vain;
The promises my youth believed—
    The smiles it sighed to gain—
The early fires that shone so bright,
    Where life's first altars were—
All—all have perished, with their light,
    And left but ashes there!

" But thou!—no change hath passed o'er thee,
    My first, my latest friend!
The same sweet tones of sympathy
    These parting hours attend,

As rose when first I woke thy strings,
 And my young heart to thee
Poured forth its yet untroubled springs,
 That flowed so fresh and free.

" Those springs are wasted, long ago,—
 Yet still, how brightly green
The old forsaken channels grow
 Where waters once have been!
So was the memory of my youth
 With thee,—though ne'er again
Could flow the founts of love and truth
 That blessed my spirit then.

" For thine have been the hopes that sprung
 Ere life had learned to grieve,—
And thine the memories fond that clung
 Around my lonely eve:—
And every voice that in my soul
 Found echoes as it passed—
The zephyr's sigh—the thunder's roll—
 The sound of breeze and blast.

"Farewell!—some mightier hand may strike
 Thy chords to prouder themes,—
Yet not to waken memories like
 To mine, of all the dreams

s

That o'er my darkened path have shed
  A briefly-glorious light,—
Like wandering stars that swiftly sped
  Across the gloom of night.

"Oh! bright, amid those early dreams,
  One glorious vision shone,—
A land of brighter flowers and streams
  Than earth had ever known,—
Where song gushed forth from golden wires,
  Like some deep river's flow,
But—all unlike our earthly lyres—
  They had no tones of woe!

"My young, my beautiful, were there—
  The loved of other years—
With locks unblanched by time or care,
  And eyes that knew not tears:
Their youth had left me, for the gloom
  Of death's eternal shade,
But in that land of changeless bloom
  I knew it could not fade!

"Oh! oft, amid the hush of night,
  That glorious land arose,—
But ever nearer to my sight
  As life drew near its close!

And now, upon the midnight air
  I hear its music swell;—
A sweeter harp awaits me, there—
  My lonely lyre—farewell!"

The song was hushed; and round the ancient ruin
  The silence of the woods hung, dim and deep,—
Save when the breeze, that came by moonlight wooing
  The latest blossoms, o'er the harp would sweep,
And wake a wild unmeasured strain, in play:—
But foresters who came, at early day,
Led by the murmurs of the tuneful wire,
Found the lone bard at rest, beside his lyre!

NOTES

TO THE MISCELLANEOUS POEMS—PART II.

'The Unsent Messenger,' p. 194.

There is a tradition of the Rabbins which says that, when Joseph was made known to his brethren, in Egypt, an Egyptian girl carried the tidings to his father; and, as a reward for the act, she was one of those allowed to enter Paradise, without death.

Note 2, page 215.

Stephens, the American traveller.

Note 3, page 223.

The Cypress of Somme is a tree of great age,—which, tradition says, was planted at the birth of Christ. It is also remarkable for a deep gash made by the sword of Francis the First, in his despair after the battle of Pavia; and for having been respected by Buonaparte—who turned from his intended track, when constructing the Road of the Simplon, in order to spare it.

Note 4, page 233.

Many astronomers suppose that the deluge was produced by the agency of a comet.

Note 5, page 233.

It is said that some of the hieroglyphics on Egyptian obelisks refer to ancient stars and comets.

Note 6, page 233.

The great comet of 1680,—which appeared when the victorious arms of the Turks threatened the destruction of Christendom.

THE END.

LONDON:
PRINTED BY J. HOLMES, 4, TOOK'S COURT,
CHANCERY LANE.